BILLY GRAHAM
Evangelistic Association
Always Good News.

Dear Friend,

I am pleased to send you this copy of *Discover Jesus in the Pages of the Bible* by Dr. Henrietta Mears. As a Bible teacher, writer, and mentor, Dr. Mears taught God's Word to thousands—and influenced many Christian leaders, including my father in his early years of ministry.

In this book, Dr. Mears explores the life of Jesus Christ as shown in the four gospels of the New Testament and explains how He fulfilled centuries of prophecy in the Old Testament. Her desire was to bring you face to face with Jesus in the pages of the Bible, and I pray that God will use her insightful look at Matthew, Mark, Luke, and John to draw you closer to our Lord and Savior. *"Blessed are those who hear the word of God and keep it!"* (Luke 11:28, NKJV).

For more than 60 years, the Billy Graham Evangelistic Association has worked to take the Good News of Jesus Christ throughout the world by every effective means available, and I'm excited about what God will do in the years ahead.

We would appreciate knowing how our ministry has touched your life. May God richly bless you.

Sincerely,

Franklin Graham
President

If you would like to know more about our ministry, please contact us:

IN THE U.S.:
Billy Graham Evangelistic Association
1 Billy Graham Parkway
Charlotte, NC 28201-0001
BillyGraham.org
info@bgea.org
Toll-free: 1-877-247-2426

IN CANADA:
Billy Graham Evangelistic
  Association of Canada
20 Hopewell Way NE
Calgary, AB T3J 5H5
BillyGraham.ca
Toll-free: 1-888-393-0003

WHAT THE Bible IS ALL ABOUT

DISCOVER JESUS

IN THE PAGES OF THE BIBLE

*Amazing Facts About the
Greatest Person Who Ever Lived*

DR. HENRIETTA C. MEARS

This *Billy Graham Library Selection* is published with
permission from Regal Books.

Regal

Published by Regal
From Gospel Light
Ventura, California, U.S.A.
www.regalbooks.com
Printed in the U.S.A.

For more information on the life of Henrietta Mears, see
Dream Big: The Henrietta Mears Story (Ventura, CA: Regal, 1990).

Library of Congress Cataloging-in-Publication Data
The Library of Congress has cataloged the first edition as follows:
Mears, Henrietta C. (Henrietta Cornelia), 1890–1963
What Jesus is all about / Henrietta C. Mears.
p. cm.
Previous ISBN 978-0-8307-6726-7
ISBN 978-1-59328-411-4
1. Jesus Christ—Person and offices. 2. Bible, N.T. Gospels—criticism, interpretation, etc. I. Title
BT203.M43 2004
232–dc22
2003024895

Rights for publishing this book outside the U.S.A. or in non-English languages are administered by Gospel Light Worldwide, an international not-for-profit ministry. For additional information, please visit www.glww.org, email info@glww.org, or write to Gospel Light Worldwide, 1957 Eastman Avenue, Ventura, CA 93003, U.S.A.

Contents

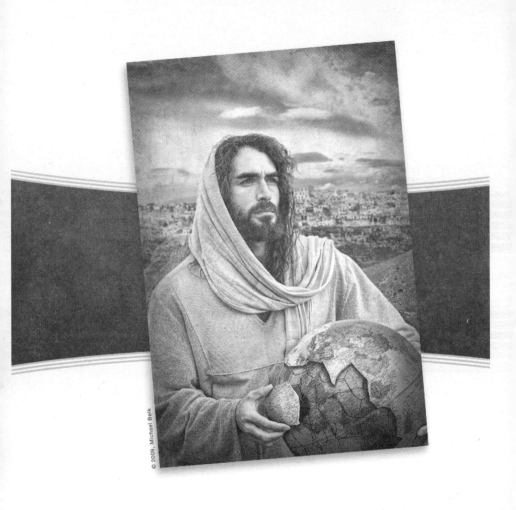

© 2009, Michael Belk

Cover image, "The Promise," made available from the
Journeys with the Messiah collection of fine art photography
depicting the messages of Jesus.

Foreword

Dr. Billy Graham

Millions of people today are searching for a reliable voice of authority. The Word of God is the only real authority we have. His Word sheds light on human nature, world problems and human suffering. But beyond that, it clearly reveals the way to God.

The message of the Bible is the message of Jesus Christ, who said, "I am the way, the truth, and the life" (John 14:6, *KJV*). It is the story of salvation; the story of your redemption and mine through Christ; the story of life, of peace, of eternity.

It is in the Holy Scriptures that we find the answers to life's ultimate questions: Where did I come from? Why am I here? Where am I going? What is the purpose of my existence?

One of the greatest needs in the Church today is to come back to the Scriptures as the basis of authority and to study them prayerfully in dependence on the Holy Spirit. When we read God's Word, we fill our hearts with His words, and God is speaking to us.

William Lyon Phelps, called the most beloved professor in America, and one-time president of Yale University, made the oft-quoted statement, "I thoroughly believe in a university education for both men and women; but I believe a knowledge of the Bible without a college course is more valuable than a college course without the Bible."

One of the greatest tragedies today is that, although the Bible is an available, open book, it is a closed book to millions—either because they leave it unread or because they read it without applying its teachings to themselves. No greater tragedy can befall a person or a nation than that of paying lip service to a Bible left unread or to a way of life not followed. The Bible, the greatest document available for the human race, needs to be opened, read and believed. This book, *Discover Jesus in the Pages of the Bible*, will help make the reading and study of God's Word interesting, challenging and useful. We commend it to you.

Foreword

By Franklin Graham

The world we are living in has changed so much in the past sixty years since Henrietta Mears first wrote *What the Bible Is All About.* She had a deep desire to help those who longed to understand the Bible better. My father has written that, in the early years of his preaching ministry, Dr. Mears was instrumental in his spiritual growth.

The majority of young people today know little or nothing about God and His Word and rarely, if ever, attend church. They don't know that God created them, loves them and sent His Son to die for their sins.

But the Word of God is always living and active, sharp and powerful, cutting through to the very soul of man (see Hebrews 4:12). I believe with all my heart that "the gospel . . . is the power of God that brings salvation" (Romans 1:16). I believe in the transforming power of that gospel that turns us from our wicked ways and makes us new creatures in Christ.

A book like this one, taken from Dr. Mears's classic, can help to open the Scriptures to those who sincerely seek truth. When we discover Jesus in the pages of the Bible, we see the reality of God's love. He sent His Son into this world to replace doubt, darkness and despair with the assurance of His love to all who will receive Him, with the promise of forgiveness of sin to repentant hearts through His shed blood on the cross, and with hope of eternal joy in His presence.

Our hope is not in things, but in God's salvation. Our hope does not come from the world, but from Jesus Christ. It is my prayer that this excerpt of Dr. Mears's book will do for many more what the original book has done for decades—point them to God's Word and to the Savior of the world, the Lord Jesus Christ.

Introduction

Few people would disagree that Jesus of Nazareth is the most famous, most popular, most revered and most important person who has ever lived on this planet. For this reason alone, it makes sense to find out about who Jesus is and what He stands for.

For the most part, wherever we go, whenever people find out about Jesus—whether through the Bible, radio, literature or film—they are almost irresistibly attracted to Him. They want to find out more. They desire to have Jesus on their side. They want to appropriate Jesus in some way, to show how Jesus would fit with their most deeply held values. They instinctively recognize the goodness and truth of Jesus' teachings; and they appreciate that Jesus was in some way especially connected to what is ultimately real.

This is true across every cultural, ethnic and religious tradition. It doesn't matter what continent, tribe or clan people are from or whether they are Hindus, Buddhists, Muslims, Taoists, animists or Marxists! Although not every person is attracted to Jesus, the multitudes are.

Even Jewish people are taking another look at Jesus today. This is somewhat surprising, because Jewish people may very well have ample reasons to avoid the issue of Jesus due to the long history of Christian persecution of Jews in the West. Nevertheless, notable Jewish writers are recognizing a sympathetic figure in the Jesus of the first century. Jesus was a Jewish person, much like them, who revered the Scriptures, operated in the prophetic tradition and endured unjust persecution. This new, positive attitude is something that was nearly unheard of only a generation or two ago.

A WORLD RELIGION

For hundreds of years, the knowledge of Jesus was pretty much confined to portions of the Middle East and the backwaters of

Europe. Great civilizations in the East, Asia, Africa and the Americas rose and fell, oblivious to Jesus' person and message. Little beachheads of sold-out Jesus communities of faith were established in some of these areas, but the majority of people never had an opportunity to hear about Him.

In the past 400 years, however, the picture has changed drastically. Both working with and against many factors (intellectual movements, science, explorative discoveries, development of trade routes, colonialism, slavery, wars, Christian missions, and so on), Christianity is the first religion to truly establish itself worldwide.

However, merely recognizing Christianity as a world religion doesn't answer the question as to why Jesus is almost universally popular. To answer that question, we need to examine the main source of Christian faith. If we want to know about Jesus, we will need to start with the Bible—in particular, the Gospels.

THE GOSPELS

The Gospels—Matthew, Mark, Luke and John—are literature, but they are unique to all of world literature.

The Gospels are solidly grounded in actual historical events, but they are not history in the modern sense of pinpointing an exact sequence of events. They contain dialogues, but they are not merely give-and-take conversations that teach us precise thinking or a particular religious path. They contain speeches that move people both rationally and emotionally, but they do not focus on techniques of persuasion. They contain miracle stories, but they are not mythological. They teach morals, but they have nothing to do with giving us a moralistic rule book. They contain the greatest love story ever told, but they are not romance novels.

Then what *is* the intended purpose of the first four books of the New Testament? What is Jesus all about?

When we read the Gospels, we are not just reading about a dead guy who lived 2,000 years ago who said and did a lot of nice things. The Gospels are intended to bring us face-to-face with the living person of Jesus Christ.

In other words, when Jesus heals the blind man, we are in the crowd, or we are the blind man who now sees.

When Jesus walks on water, we are with the disciples on the boat, drenched by rowdy waves, scared witless and wondering what's going on. When Jesus says, "I am the bread of life" (John 6:35), we have to figure out what in the world He's talking about. When Jesus urges us, "Follow Me" (Matthew 4:19; Mark 1:17), we have a personal and existential choice to make—to allow the living Jesus into our lives, which brings spiritual birth into our hearts and transforms us by His presence, or to keep going our own way.

In short, in all of human literature, there is nothing that compares with the Gospels, because there is no one who rivals the living Jesus. He knows the human condition better than anyone else.

Who needs a role model? Who desires truth, beauty and goodness? Who has sorrow? Who needs forgiveness for doing selfish and wrongful acts? Who needs healing—psychological, physical and spiritual? Who needs meaning in life, whether things are good or have gone dreadfully bad? Who needs unconditional love and a place to belong?

We all do. We need to allow Jesus to meet us at our point of need. As we read the Gospels, let's allow Jesus to do His work in our lives. It will be a good and beautiful work.

Remember, it's not always an easy road. We're going to have to put some sandals on and get dusty with Jesus on the rocky trails of Galilee; but as we do, we'll see how Jesus treats women, children, sick people and outcasts with the utmost respect and dignity. We'll be struck by His tenderness and surprised by His fierceness. We might even shout in shock or fear—or taste salty tears of joy—at His miracles. Let us entertain the possibility that maybe, just maybe, this same Jesus will meet us in the way He met people in the first century.

HENRIETTA MEARS

Henrietta Mears wrote *What the Bible Is All About*, on which this book is based. Mears was one of the most remarkable Christian women of the twentieth century. Born in North Dakota in 1890, she came to California in 1928 to become the director of Christian education at Hollywood Presbyterian Church. She stayed at Hollywood Presbyterian until her death in 1963. During her ministry, she gained worldwide recognition and prominence.

Henrietta Mears was a multitalented, godly woman. Among other things, she taught the college class at Hollywood Presbyterian; oversaw the production of an entirely new Sunday School approach, which in turn led to the formation of Gospel Light Publications and Regal Books; influenced many of the twentieth century's greatest male Christian leaders through conferences and personal contacts; spearheaded the Forest Home Christian Camp; and founded Gospel Light Worldwide, a nonprofit organization dedicated to translating the best of Christian literature into foreign languages.

One of her most wonderful legacies is her book *What the Bible Is All About*. The book is a condensation of teachings she developed for high school students in the 1930s. It continues to sell tens of thousands of copies each year.

This book introduces some of Henrietta Mears's teachings—those on Jesus—to a new generation of readers. It also includes study questions for each Gospel. Throughout the book, you'll notice that selected Scriptures are contained within callouts. These Scripture passages are highlighted because they are either Old Testament prophecies fulfilled by Jesus or they are an Old Testament passage(s) describing a promise and a New Testament passage describing how Jesus fulfilled the given promise.

SOME TIPS FOR BEGINNERS

For those who may be new to Bible reading, new to Jesus or new to the Christian faith—maybe just checking out "this Jesus thing"—that's okay. Everybody has to start somewhere. The following are some tips for you to consider as you begin your reading of this book and the Gospels.

Ask God to Lead You

Before you begin, ask God to lead you and guide you as you go through the material. It's never a bad idea to ask God—the source of all wisdom—for a little piece of wisdom.

Read this Book Alongside an Open Bible

In the pages of this book Henrietta Mears will be constantly asking you to look up Bible verses and passages, and if you do so you will gain immeasurably from the exercise. It takes patience and perseverance to look up all the passages referenced in this book. Mears believed in teaching key concepts through repetition, so sometimes she asks you to look up the same verses several times.

If you feel things are progressing too slowly, don't feel like you must look up every single reference. Just look up the ones that will help you understand. Maybe you can take a pencil and check those you look up; then look up the others later if you have the time and inclination.

Keep a Bible Concordance Nearby

As you read this book, you might want to look up certain words in a Bible concordance (an alphabetical list of all of the principal words in the Bible). This Bible study aid will help you find where words occur in the Bible, and it is a great tool if you want to see how one word is used in different contexts. Nowadays, you can find Bible concordances online, which work even better than book concordances because of their extensive search capabilities.

Now it's time to discover what Jesus is all about!

Bayard Taylor
Theological Editor

Key Events of the Gospels

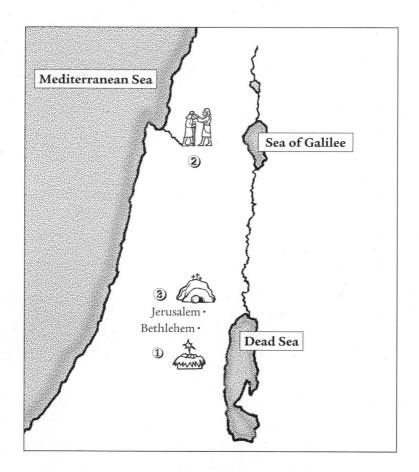

The Gospels: The Person of Jesus Christ

The Gospels record the ① birth, life, miracles, healing ministry ②, teachings, death and resurrection ③ of Jesus Christ. Each Gospel has a slightly different purpose and audience, but together they give us an amazingly clear picture of who Jesus Christ was in His earthly ministry, and they invite us to believe in the Savior of the world (see John 4:42) who conquered sin, Satan and death on the cross.

The Holy Land at the Time of Jesus

SIDON
ITURAEA · ABILENE
SAREPTA · DAMASCUS
TYRE · MT. HERMON
· CAESAREA PHILIPPI
PHOENICIA · TRACHONITIS

MEDITERRANEAN
SEA
GALILEE · GAULANITIS
CHORAZIN
PTOLEMAIS · CAPERNAUM · BETHSAIDA
CANA · SEA OF
MAGDALA · GALILEE
RIVER TIBERIAS
KISHON · NAZARETH · GERGESA?
RIVER · MT. OF
KISHON · BEATITUDES · GADARA
· NAIN · RIVER · DECAPOLIS
· JORDAN
CAESAREA · SALIM?
AENON?
· SAMARIA

SAMARIA
PLAIN OF · SYCHAR
SHARON · MT. GERIZIM

ANTIPATRIS · BETHABARA?
JOPPA · ARIMATHEA
EPHRAIM · PERAEA
LYDDA · RAMAH
· EMMAUS · JERICHO
BETHPHAGE? · BETHANY?
AZOTUS · JERUSALEM · MT. OF OLIVES
BETHANY ·
BETHLEHEM
JUDAEA · DEAD SEA
· GAZA

IDUMAEA
EGYPT
ARABIA

Understanding
the Gospels

The Gospels Portray Jesus Christ,
Our Savior and Lord

Dr. Henry Van Dyke, a turn-of-the-twentieth-century minister and professor of English literature at Princeton, once said:

> If four witnesses should appear before a judge to give an account of a certain event, and each should tell exactly the same story in the same words, the judge would probably conclude, not that their testimony was exceptionally valuable, but that the only event which was certain beyond a doubt was that they had agreed to tell the same story. But if each man had told what he had seen, as he had seen it, then the evidence would be credible. And when we read the four Gospels, is not that exactly what

we find? The four men tell the same story each in his own way.

The word "gospel" is derived from the two Anglo-Saxon words "God," meaning "good," and "spell," meaning "tidings" or "history." The four writers of the Gospels are called "evangelists," from a Greek word meaning "bringer of good tidings." The first three Gospels—Matthew, Mark and Luke—are called the Synoptic Gospels, because, unlike John's Gospel, they give a synopsis of Christ's life. The word "synopsis" is derived from two Greek words meaning "a view together, a collective view." So these three Gospels may be viewed together.

The Synoptic Gospels are striking in their similarities: He is here! The promised One has come! The One whom all the prophets have foretold, Jesus Christ, the Lord. They are equally striking in their differences:

- The Synoptics chiefly tell about Christ's ministry in Galilee—John's Gospel tells of Christ's ministry in Judea.

- The Synoptics tell about Christ's miracles, parables and addresses to the multitudes—John's Gospel relates Christ's deeper and more abstract discourses, His conversations and His prayers.

- The Synoptics portray Christ in action—John's Gospel portrays Christ in meditation and communion.

Every prophet in the Old Testament assured God's Chosen People again and again that a Messiah would come who would be the King of the Jews. They therefore looked forward with passionate longing and patriotism to the coming of that King in pomp and power. Expect to find this King in the Gospels "the one Moses wrote about in the Law, and about whom the prophets also wrote—Jesus" (John 1:45). But know that you will find Him infinitely more beautiful in person than any prophet's vision of Him.

We read in Isaiah 7:14: "Therefore the Lord himself will give you a sign: The virgin will conceive and give birth to a son, and will call him Immanuel" (the name "Immanuel" means "God with us"). This is the One the evangelists tell us about—Jesus who lived with us. John says, "The Word became flesh and made his dwelling among us" (John 1:14). Think of God coming down to live with people! It seems the Gospels are the center of the whole Bible. All that the prophets said leads us to our Lord's earthly life and work, and all that follows in the Epistles proceeds from them. They tell us *when* and *how* Christ came; the Epistles tell us *why* and *for what* Christ came. Notice where the four Gospels are placed in the Bible—they stand at the close of the Old Testament and before the Epistles. The Gospels are at the center of everything.

Dr. William H. Griffith Thomas, a turn-of-the-twentieth-century American New Testament scholar, suggested that we remember four words to help us link together the whole of God's revelation:

- "Preparation"—In the Old Testament, God makes ready for the coming of the Messiah.
- "Manifestation"—In the four Gospels, Christ enters the world, dies for the world and founds His Church.
- "Appropriation"—In the Acts and Epistles, the ways are revealed in which the Lord Jesus was received, appropriated and applied in individual lives.
- "Consummation"—In the book of Revelation, the outcome of God's perfect plan through Christ is revealed.

THE MEANING OF "GOSPEL"

"Gospel" means "good news." The good news concerning Jesus, the Son of God, is given to us by four writers—Matthew, Mark, Luke and John. There is only one gospel—the glad story of salvation through Jesus Christ our Lord. But we are given four pictures of Christ. The combined Gospels present a personality rather than a connected story of a life.

The word "gospel" is never used in the New Testament as a reference to a book. It always means "good news." When we speak of the Gospel of Luke, we ought to understand that it means the good news of Jesus Christ as recorded by Luke. Nevertheless, from the earliest times, the term "gospel" has been applied to each of the four narratives that record the life of Christ.

No doubt, originally the good news was oral. Men went from one place to another, telling the glad story by word of mouth. After a while, a written record was necessary. Evidently, more than one person attempted to write everything down, but nothing was successfully completed. See what Luke says in Luke 1:1-4:

> Many have undertaken to draw up an account of the things that have been fulfilled among us, just as they were handed down to us by those who from the first were eyewitnesses and servants of the word. With this in mind, since I myself have carefully investigated everything from the beginning, I too decided to write an orderly account for you, most excellent Theophilus, so that you may know the certainty of the things you have been taught.

FOUR GOSPELS INSTEAD OF ONE

As everyone knows, there are four Gospels, but this fact has given rise to several questions: Why four? Why wouldn't one straightforward, continuous narrative have been enough? Wouldn't this have been simpler and clearer? Wouldn't this have saved us from some of the difficulties that have arisen because of what some have said are conflicting accounts?

A Complete Picture of Christ

The answer seems plain: Because one or two would not have given us a well-rounded and complete picture of the life of Christ. It is true that each of the four Gospels has much in common with the others: Each deals with Christ's earthly ministry, His death and resurrection, His teachings and miracles; but each Gospel is also different because four distinct offices of Christ are portrayed in the Gospels:

1. King in Matthew
2. Servant in Mark
3. Son of man in Luke
4. Son of God in John

There are deliberate gaps that none of the evangelists attempts to fill in. For instance, all omit any account of the 18 years of Christ's life between the ages of 12 and 30. And although each Gospel is complete in itself, each author was very selective: Only a few of Christ's miracles are described and only a portion of His teachings are given in each. Each evangelist has recorded that which is relevant and pertinent to his particular theme. For example, Matthew deliberately adds to his account what Mark omits. Read what John says in 21:25: "Jesus did many other things as well. If every one of them were written down, I suppose that even the whole world would not have room for the books that would be written."

In the National Gallery in London, on a single canvas there are three portraits of Charles I. In one, his head is turned to the right; in another, to the left; and in the center is a full-face view. This odd "portrait" was painted by the Flemish painter Anthony Van Dyck for the Roman sculptor Giovanni Lorenzo Bernini, who planned to make a bust of the king. By combining the impressions he received, Bernini was better able to produce a faithful likeness. One view would not have been enough.

It may be true that the Gospels were intended to serve a purpose similar to that of those portraits. Each presents a different aspect of our Lord's life on earth. When the Gospels are viewed together, we have the complete picture. He was a King, but He was the perfect Servant, too. He was the Son of man, but we must not forget that He was the Son of God.

There are four Gospels with one Christ, four accounts with one purpose, and four sketches of one person.

The Significance of Four Gospels

Let us present another explanation for why there are four Gospels instead of one: Four is an earthly number. Scriptures explain many things for us, and many people believe that the Scriptures use numbers with precision, accuracy and real meaning:

- Seven is the perfect number.
- Three is the number of the Godhead.
- Forty is the number of testing.
- Four is the number of the earth. There are four points of the compass (north, east, south, west). There are four seasons (spring, summer, autumn, winter). In the parable of the sower, Jesus divided the field into four kinds of soil. Later He said, "The field is the world" (Matthew 13:38).

If four is the earth number, how fitting that the Holy Spirit should have given us four Gospels in which to depict the earthly ministry of the heavenly One.

The Fulfillment of Prophecy

The Gospels are bound up with the promises of the Messiah in the Old Testament. We cannot explain the Gospels apart from the great messianic prophecies in the Old Testament. The prophets portrayed a magnificent picture of the Messiah. They told of His offices, mission, birth, suffering, death, resurrection and glory. Let us consider the four names and/or titles the prophets bestowed upon Him:

- King (see Psalm 72; Isaiah 9:6-7; 32:1; Jeremiah 23:5; Zechariah 9:9; 14:9)—These passages, among many others, tell of the kingly office of the Messiah. The prophets told much of His kingdom and its extent, and of Christ's ultimate triumph.
- The servant of Jehovah (see Isaiah 42:1-7; 52:13-15; 53)
- The man, the Son of man (see Genesis 3:15; 22:18; Isaiah 7:14-16; 9:6)
- God (see Isaiah 9:6; 40:3-5; 47:4; Jeremiah 23:6)

As these four, Jesus is set forth in the Gospels.

FULFILLED OLD TESTAMENT PROPHECIES OF CHRIST JESUS

AS KING:

He is the one who will build a house for my Name, and I will establish the throne of his kingdom forever. I will be his father, and he will be my son. . . . I will punish him with the rod of men, with floggings inflicted by men.

2 SAMUEL 7:13-14

For to us a child is born, to us a son is given, and the government will be on his shoulders. And he will be called Wonderful Counselor, Mighty God, Everlasting Father, Prince of Peace.

ISAIAH 9:6

AS SERVANT:

Here is my servant, whom I uphold, my chosen one in whom I delight; I will put my Spirit on him and he will bring justice to the nations.

ISAIAH 42:1

But he was pierced for our transgressions, he was crushed for our iniquities; the punishment that brought us peace was upon him, and by his wounds we are healed.

ISAIAH 53:5

AS SON OF MAN:

In my vision at night I looked, and there before me was one like a son of man, coming with the clouds of heaven. He approached the Ancient of Days and was led into his presence. He was given authority, glory and sovereign power; all peoples, nations and men of every language worshiped him. His dominion is an everlasting dominion that will not pass away, and his kingdom is one that will never be destroyed.

ISAIAH 42:1

JESUS IN THE FOUR GOSPELS

Master this outline and you will be familiar with the contents of the Gospels for life:

1. King—Matthew presents Jesus as King. This Gospel was written primarily for the Jew, for Jesus is the Son of David. His royal genealogy is given in Matthew 1. In Matthew 5–7, in the Sermon on the Mount, we have the King's manifesto, containing the laws of His kingdom.

2. Servant—Mark depicts Jesus as Servant. Written for the Romans, this gospel contains no genealogy. Why? People are not interested in the genealogy of a servant. More miracles are found here than in any other Gospel. Romans cared little for words and were far more interested in deeds.

3. Son of man—Luke portrays Jesus as the Son of man, the perfect man. This Gospel was written for the Greeks. Christ's genealogy is given as far back as Adam (the first man) instead of to Abraham. As a perfect Man, Christ is very often seen in prayer and with angels ministering to Him.

4. Son of God—John portrays Jesus as the Son of God. Written to all who will believe, with the purpose of leading people to Christ, this Gospel illustrates and demonstrates Christ's relationship to God and as God (see John 20:31). The opening verse causes us to go back to "the beginning" (John 1:1).

Dr. W. H. Griffith Thomas gave the pictures of the Gospels in this way:

1. Matthew is concerned with the coming of a *promised Savior.*

2. Mark is concerned with the life of a *powerful Savior.*
3. Luke is concerned with the grace of a *perfect Savior.*
4. John is concerned with the possession of a *personal Savior.*

INTENDED AUDIENCES OF THE GOSPELS

In the Gospels, Christ was going to be presented to widely different groups of people who made up the world. Each group was capable of appreciating one particular kind of presentation more than another. The four groups of people in Jesus' day also represent the four types of people today.

1. The Jewish People Had Special Training

They were steeped in the Old Testament Scripture and the prophets. Matthew writes the story of Jesus' life on earth especially for these people. If Jewish people were to be impressed with Jesus, they would need to be taught by somebody who understood their customs and way of thinking. Jewish people needed to know that this Jesus came to fulfill the prophecies of the Old Testament. Over and over again we read in Matthew that an action or some words of Christ "fulfilled" what the Lord had said through a prophet.

We have the same type of people today. They revel in prophecies fulfilled and unfulfilled. They want to know what the prophets spoke and how prophecies are being fulfilled.

2. The Romans Were Masters of the World at that Time

Mark wrote especially for Romans. The Romans knew nothing about Old Testament Scriptures. They were not interested in prophecy being fulfilled. But they were vitally concerned about a remarkable leader who had appeared in Judea. He had claimed more than ordinary authority and had possessed extraordinary powers. They wanted to hear more about this Jesus—what sort of a person He really was, what He had said and what He had done.

The Romans liked Mark's straightforward message. The word "and" is used in Mark 1,375 times (in the *KJV*); and its use helps to smoothly move this narrative along. Mark's Gospel is filled with deeds, not words. Clearly it is the Gospel of the ministry of Christ.

The Romans of Jesus' day were like average businesspeople are today. They are not concerned about the genealogy of a king but with a God "who is able," a God who can *do* things and meet a person's every need. Mark is the businessperson's Gospel.

3. The Greeks Were Lovers of Beauty, Poetry and Culture

The Greeks lived in a world of large ideas. Their tastes were fastidious. The Gospel of Luke (the Greek doctor who wrote to his own countrymen) tells of the birth and childhood of Jesus. It gives the inspired songs connected with the life of Christ. We find Elizabeth's greeting when Mary visited her (see Luke 1:42-45). We can almost hear the song of the virgin mother and Zacharias's burst into praise when speech was restored to him (see Luke 1:46-55,68-79). At the Savior's birth, a chorus of angel voices ring out (see Luke 2:13-14), and then the shepherd's song of praise to God is heard (see Luke 2:20).

The Greeks of Jesus' day are like the students and idealists today who seek truth, because they believe that truth is the means to happiness.

4. All the Other People in the World Made up the Fourth Group

John's Gospel is written to all people everywhere so that they might believe that Jesus is the Christ. Christ is portrayed as the Son of God. This Gospel is filled with extraordinary claims that prove Jesus' divine character and mission.

The "all people everywhere" of John's day are like the masses today who need Christ. They include the "whoever" who will believe in the Lord Jesus because they have a sense of need and want to receive the gift of eternal life through Jesus Christ the Lord (John 3:16).

KEYS TO THE GOSPELS

Front-Door Keys

God has hung the key to the Gospel of Matthew right over the entrance. The book opens with: "This is the genealogy of Jesus the Messiah the son of David, the son of Abraham" (Matthew 1:1). This shows Jesus' covenant position as the Son of Abraham (see Genesis 12:1-3; Galatians 3:16) and His royal position as Son of David. Matthew presents Christ as King; he gives the royal genealogy in the first 17 verses. A king is not chosen by popular ballot but by birth.

Turn now to Mark. See how this book opens. No genealogy is given. The reason is that Jesus is portrayed as a Servant, and no one is interested in the pedigree of a servant.

Turn to Luke. Is a genealogy given? See Luke 3:23. Matthew traces Christ's line back to Abraham and David to show that Jesus was a Jew and of the royal line. Luke traces Jesus' line back to Adam, the first man. Christ is presented as the ideal man. He was of the line of Adam.

Turn to John. How does this book open? No genealogy but "in the beginning was the Word, and the Word was with God, and the Word was God" (John 1:1). John portrays Christ as God.

Back-Door Keys

Now let us see how the Gospels close. Turn to Matthew 28:18-20, the King's command and commission to His disciples: "All authority in heaven and on earth has been given to me. Therefore go and make disciples of all nations, baptizing them in the name of the Father and of the Son and of the Holy Spirit, and teaching them to obey everything I have commanded you. And surely I am with you always, to the very end of the age." The Messiah is still on earth, for it is on earth and not in heaven that the Son of David will reign in glory.

Now look at the close of Mark: "Then the disciples went out and preached everywhere, and the Lord worked with them and confirmed his word by the signs that accompanied it" (Mark

16:20). This is very significant and appropriate. Jesus, the Servant, is pictured as still laboring with His disciples.

Luke ends in a different way. Notice what Luke says in 24:51: "While he was blessing them, he left them and was taken up into heaven." Jesus, the perfect man, is ascending to the Father.

The closing verse of John is also significant: "Jesus did many other things as well. If every one of them were written down, I suppose that even the whole world would not have room for the books that would be written" (John 21:25). Truly, "No one ever spoke the way this man does," for He was the true Son of God (John 7:46).

2

Understanding Matthew

Matthew Portrays Jesus Christ, the Promised Messiah

SELECTED BIBLE READINGS

DAY OF THE WEEK		MAIN TOPIC
Sunday: Matthew 1:18–2:23	The King Is Born	
Monday: Matthew 4	The King Begins Work	
Tuesday: Matthew 5:1-17,41-48; 6:19-34	The King States Kingdom Laws	
Wednesday: Matthew 10:1-33	The King Commissions His Followers	
Thursday: Matthew 13:1-52	The King Explains the Kingdom	
Friday: Matthew 21:1-11	The King Offers Himself as King	
Saturday: Matthew 25:14-16	The King Will Return	

AUTHOR: This gospel is known as the Gospel of Matthew because, according to Church tradition from at least the second century AD, the apostle Matthew wrote it. The style of the book is exactly what would be expected of a man who was once a tax collector. Matthew has a keen interest in accounting, and the book is very orderly and concise (see Matthew 18:23-24; 25:14-15).

DATE: As an apostle, Matthew wrote this book during the early period of the Church, possibly AD 50 or earlier, when the gospel was only preached to Jewish people and not yet to Gentiles (see Acts 11:19). This was a time when most Christians were Jewish messianic believers, so Matthew's focus is on the Jewish perspective of Jesus as the Messiah promised to the Jewish people.

PURPOSE AND SUMMARY: This Gospel is the most complete account of Jesus' teachings and was written to convince the writer's Jewish audience that Jesus was the Messiah descended from David, the One promised by the Old Testament prophets. The most significant teaching passages in the Gospel of Matthew are the Sermon on the Mount (5–7) and the parable sections of the book (especially chapter 13).

GENERAL CHARACTERISTICS OF MATTHEW'S GOSPEL

Matthew has a special goal in his Gospel: to show the Jews that Jesus is the long-expected Messiah, the Son of David, and that His life fulfilled the Old Testament prophecies. The purpose is given in the first verse: "This is the genealogy of Jesus the Messiah the son of David, the son of Abraham." This statement links Christ to the two great covenants God made with David and Abraham. God's covenant with David consisted of the promise of a King to sit upon his throne forever (see 2 Samuel 7:8-13). God's covenant with Abraham promised that through him all families of the earth would be blessed (see Genesis 12:3). David's son was a King. Abraham's son was a Sacrifice. Matthew opens with the birth of a King and closes with the offering of a Sacrifice.

From the beginning, Jesus is associated with the Jewish nation. Matthew was wise not to alienate the Jews who might read the story. He wants to convince them that Jesus fulfilled every prophecy concerning their promised Messiah. He quotes freely from the Old Testament more than any of the other evangelists. Twenty-nine such quotations are given. Thirteen times he says that this or that event "took place to fulfill what the Lord had said through the prophet" (Matthew 1:22).

It is difficult for us to appreciate what the Jews thought Matthew was actually asking them to do. It seemed to the Jews that according to Matthew, they must give up their traditions and orthodoxy and accept another creed. But Matthew (and Paul, especially in Galatians) shows the Jewish believers in Jesus that they were not being told to give up their old faith; rather, they only had to give up symbols and shadows for real substance.

Matthew was well acquainted with Jewish history and customs. He speaks of farming and fishing and the housekeeping of his people in the seven parables in chapter 13. He knew this intimate record would strike responsive chords in the hearts of the Jewish people.

As you read Matthew, get a clear and comprehensive view of the entire Gospel. Keep in mind the messianic character of this Gospel. Note the balance between Jesus' ministry and teaching. We find the genealogy of the King; His birth in Bethlehem, the city of David, according to Micah's prophecy (see Micah 5:2); the coming of the forerunner, John the Baptist, as Malachi had predicted (see Malachi 3:1); the ministry of the King; His rejection by Israel; and the promise of His coming again in power and glory.

The Author

The author is no doubt a Jewish believer in Jesus (see Matthew 9:9; 10:3). Matthew, whose name means "gift of the Lord," was a tax collector at Capernaum when Jesus chose him as one of the 12 disciples. His name is found in all the lists of the 12, though Mark and Luke give his other name, Levi. The only word the author speaks about himself is that he was a "publican" (*KJV*), which was then a derogatory term, similar to the word "politician" as it is sometimes used today. The other evangelists tell about the great feast Matthew gave Jesus, and they record the significant fact that Matthew left behind all he had and followed Jesus. No doubt he was a man of means.

Matthew breaks the silence of 400 years between Malachi's prophecy and the announcement of the birth of Jesus. Israel was under the domination of the Roman Empire. No man of "the house of David" had been allowed to sit upon the throne for 600 years.

The Royal Line

Herod was not the king of Israel but a governor of Judea, appointed by the emperor of Rome. The man who really had the right to the throne of the house of David was Joseph, the carpenter, who became the husband of Mary. See the genealogy of Joseph in Matthew 1, and notice especially one name, Jeconiah, in verse 11. If Joseph had been Jesus' father according to the flesh, Jesus could never have occupied the throne, because what God's Word says made that impossible: There had been a curse on this royal line since the days of Jeconiah. In Jeremiah 22:30 we read, "This is what the LORD says: 'Record this man as if childless, a man who will not prosper in his lifetime, for none of his offspring will prosper, none will sit on the throne of David or rule anymore in Judah.' " Joseph was in the line of this curse. Therefore, if Christ had been Joseph's son, He could not have sat on David's throne.

But we find another genealogy in Luke 3. This is Mary's line back to David through Nathan, not Jeconiah (see Luke 3:31). There was no curse on this line. To Mary, God said, "Do not be afraid, Mary; you have found favor with God. You will conceive and give birth to a son, and you are to call him Jesus. He will be great and will be called the Son of the Most High. The Lord God will give him the throne of his father David, and he will reign over Jacob's descendants forever; his kingdom will never end" (Luke 1:30-33).

The Book

The book of Matthew follows after the Old Testament and is the beginning of the New. It is the connecting link between the two parts of the Bible. It is written for the Jews and it is fittingly placed. It takes for granted that the course of events up to this point is known to its readers. The Old Testament had closed with the chosen nation looking for their long-promised King, their Messiah. Now the silence is broken and the coming of the Messiah declared. Matthew's Gospel shows that Jesus was that King. It is the Gospel of fulfillment.

Matthew emphasizes the Jewish side of Lord Jesus. Only in this Gospel do we find a record of the Messiah's declaration, "I was sent only to the lost sheep of Israel" (Matthew 15:24). What did His own people do with Him? Read John 1:11.

In numerical position, the book of Matthew is the fortieth in the canon. Forty is always a number of testing, or evaluation, in Scripture:

- Jesus was tempted by the devil for 40 days.
- Israel was in the wilderness for 40 years.
- David was king for 40 years.
- Moses was in a palace for 40 years, and then he was in a desert for 40 years.

What other instances of this number 40 do you remember in Scripture? Look the number up in your concordance.

In this fortieth book of the Bible, Israel's response to the presence of the Messiah is being tested. Christ is presented as King to the Jews, but most of the religious leaders rejected Him—not only as their Messiah, but also as their Savior (see Matthew 16:21).

MATTHEW 1–2: BIRTH OF THE KING

Matthew is the Gospel of the Messiah, God's anointed One. The main purpose of the Spirit in this book is to show that Jesus of Nazareth is the predicted Messiah, the Deliverer of whom Moses and the prophets wrote, "whose origins are from of old, from ancient times" (Micah 5:2). He is the child that was to be born, the Son given, of whom Isaiah said, "will be called Wonderful Counselor, Mighty God, Everlasting Father, Prince of Peace" (Isaiah 9:6).

The Record of Jesus' Birth

Jesus "was born in Bethlehem of Judea, during the time of King Herod" (Matthew 2:1; see also Micah 5:2). We know this place and this king. We don't have to pretend that this place or this person existed. Christianity is a historical religion. The Gospel does not begin with "Once upon a time" but starts with "Bethlehem in Judea" (Matthew 2:1). The town is there, so we can visit the actual place where Jesus was born. Herod was a real person, because ancient historians wrote about him and archaeologists have found proof of him. There is nothing mythical about this monster of iniquity.

Matthew's statements are facts and no critic or unbeliever can doubt them. The Gospel narrative sets its record in the solid foundation of history. We are not building our faith on a myth but on substantial fact. These events did not happen in a dark corner but in the broad daylight, and the entire book is not afraid of the geographer's map and the historian's pen.

The story of the birth of Jesus in Matthew differs from the record in Luke, but they complement each other. While there is much untold, God *has* told us all that we need to know. Jesus' earthly life began in a stable. His cradle was a manger. His family and friends were humble people. He was born as a helpless babe. How human was our Lord! But Jesus was announced by an archangel, welcomed by an angel choir and worshiped by earth's wisest philosophers (the Magi)! How divine was our Lord!

OLD TESTAMENT PROMISE AND NEW TESTAMENT FULFILLMENT

Therefore the Lord himself will give you a sign: The virgin will be with child and will give birth to a son, and will call him Immanuel.

ISAIAH 7:14

All this took place to fulfill what the Lord had said through the prophet: "The virgin will be with child and will give birth to a son, and they will call him Immanuel"—which means, "God with us."

MATTHEW 1:22-23

The History of Jesus' Line

When you begin reading Matthew and Luke, the repetition of "the father of" (Matthew 1:1-17) and "the son of" (Luke 3:23-38) may make you wonder if these lists are worth reading. You need to realize that if they were included in Scripture, they were put there for a purpose. At this point, we want to look at these two genealogies.

A genealogy is the history of the descent of an individual or family from an ancestor. The two genealogies of Christ given by Matthew and Luke are not alike, however, because each author has a different goal in mind as he traces the descent of Christ:

- Matthew traces Jesus' line back to Abraham and David to show that He was a Jew (coming from David)—Luke traces Jesus' line back to Adam to show that He belonged to the human race.

- Matthew shows Jesus as of royal descent, the King, the Messiah, the lion of the tribe of Judah, the promised ruler of Israel—Luke shows that Jesus has a human lineage; He is the ideal man, born of woman.

You will find that these pictures of Jesus are maintained all through each Gospel—Matthew portraying Jesus as the Messiah; Luke, as the man.

Why are we concerned about these genealogies? Because they give us the key to the whole life of Christ. They show us from the very start that He was not just another man but that He was descended from a royal family, and there was a king's blood in His veins. If He were not a King, He could not claim the rulership of our lives. If He were not a man, He could not know "our pain" and be acquainted with "our suffering" (Isaiah 53:4).

Go through Matthew and follow this trail of the King:

1. The King's name—"They will call him Immanuel" (Matthew 1:23).

2. The King's position—"For out of you will come a ruler who will shepherd my people Israel" (Matthew 2:6).

3. The King's announcement—"Prepare the way for the Lord, make straight paths for him" (Matthew 3:3).

4. The King's coronation—"This is my Son, whom I love; with him I am well pleased" (Matthew 3:17).

5. The King's due respect—"Worship the Lord your God, and serve him only" (Matthew 4:10).

6. The King's proclamation—"And he began to teach them" (Matthew 5:2). "He taught as one who had authority" (Matthew 7:29).

7. The King's loyalty—"Whoever is not with me is against me, and whoever does not gather with me scatters" (Matthew 12:30).

8. The King's enemies—"From that time on Jesus began to explain to his disciples that he must go to Jerusalem and suffer many things at the hands of the elders, the chief priests and the teachers of the law" (Matthew 16:21).

9. The King's love—"The Son of Man did not come to be served, but to serve, and to give his life as a ransom for many" (Matthew 20:28).

10. The King's glory—"When the Son of Man comes . . . then the King will say . . . 'Come, you who are blessed by my Father; take your inheritance'" (Matthew 25:31-34).

11. The King's sacrifice—"When they had crucified him . . . they placed the written charge against him: THIS IS JESUS, THE KING OF THE JEWS" (Matthew 27:35-37).

12. The King's victory—"He is not here; he has risen, just as he said" (Matthew 28:6).

OLD TESTAMENT PROMISE AND NEW TESTAMENT FULFILLMENT

But you, Bethlehem Ephrathah, though you are small among the clans of Judah, out of you will come for me one who will be ruler over Israel, whose origins are from of old, from ancient times.

MICAH 5:2

When he had called together all the people's chief priests and teachers of the law, he asked them where the Christ was to be born. "In Bethlehem in Judea," they replied, "for this is what the prophet has written."

MATTHEW 2:4-5

The Visit by the Magi

Matthew alone tells of the visit of the wise men from the East, because he alone was interested in recording the birth of a king. The wise men were Persian Magi—scholars and students of the stars. They came to worship and honor the King, not a creed. These wise men did not come asking, "Where is the one who has been born the Savior of the world?" but, "Where is the one who has been born king of the Jews?" (Matthew 2:2). This was the question on every lip. With all the prophecies that had been made to Israel, neither the world nor Israel could be criticized for expecting a king who would rule the earth from David's throne (see Jeremiah 23:3-6; 30:8-10; 33:14-16,25-26; Ezekiel 37:21; Isaiah 9:7; Hosea 3:4-5).

The adoration of the wise men foreshadowed Christ's universal dominion. Some day "every knee should bow . . . and every tongue confess that Jesus Christ is Lord, to the glory of God the Father" (Philippians 2:10-11). "May he rule from sea to sea and from the River to the ends of the earth" (Psalm 72:8).

Paul tells us in Galatians 4:4-5, "When the set time had fully come, God sent his Son, born of a woman, born under the law, to redeem those under the law, that we might receive adoption to sonship." Jesus came to be the world's Savior.

The birth of Jesus was followed by 12 years of silence until His visit with the doctors in Jerusalem. Then the Gospels are silent again, with only the words "carpenter's son" (Matthew 13:55) or "carpenter" (Mark 6:3) to throw any light on the next 18 years and to let us know what He was doing. Jesus took 30 years of preparation for three years of ministry.

OLD TESTAMENT PROMISE AND NEW TESTAMENT FULFILLMENT

I will proclaim the decree of the lord: He said to me, "You are my Son; today I have become your Father."

PSALM 2:7

And a voice from heaven said, "This is my Son, whom I love; with him I am well pleased."

MATTHEW 2:4-5

MATTHEW 3–16:20: PROCLAMATION OF THE KINGDOM

John the Baptist had another name. As the prophet Isaiah began to unfold the real message of his book—the coming of the Messiah, servant of Jehovah—he introduced a character known simply as "a voice": "a voice of one calling: 'In the wilderness prepare the way for the LORD; make straight in the desert a highway for our God'" (Isaiah 40:3). This voice, although unnamed in Isaiah, is to announce the coming of Jesus Christ. His two functions—that of voice and that of messenger—are all that the Old Testament tells us of John the Baptist (see Malachi 3:1). But it actually tells us a lot. It is indeed wonderful, not only that Christ should have been foretold all through the Scriptures, but also that His forerunner, John the Baptist, also is described.

In Matthew we hear the "voice": "Repent, for the kingdom of heaven has come near." This is he who was spoken of through the prophet Isaiah: "A voice of one calling in the wilderness, 'Prepare the way for the Lord, make straight paths for him'" (Matthew 3:2-3).

The King must be announced! It was the duty of this herald to go before the King, as a Roman officer before his ruler, and command that the roads be repaired over which his master would travel. John the Baptist did this. He showed that the spiritual roads of the lives of men and women and nations were full of the potholes of sin and sharp turns of sinfulness, and they needed repairing and straightening.

We see the King stepping from His personal and private life into His public ministry (see Matthew 4). He is facing a crisis. Satan met Him after He received His Father's blessing at His baptism: "This is my Son, whom I love; with him I am well pleased" (Matthew 3:17). Jesus then begins to carry out the plans for which He came into the world. He was led into the wilderness to face the first major conflict of His public ministry.

OLD TESTAMENT PROMISE AND NEW TESTAMENT FULFILLMENT

He will rule from sea to sea and from the River
to the ends of the earth.

PSALM 72:8

That at the name of Jesus every knee should bow, in heaven and
on earth and under the earth, and every tongue confess that Jesus Christ
is Lord, to the glory of God the Father.

PHILIPPIANS 2:10-11

Notice that Satan offered Jesus a shortcut to the universal Kingdom that He had come to gain through the long and painful way of the cross; but Christ came to be a Savior first and then a King. How strong is the temptation to take a shortcut to our ambitions!

Jesus stood victorious, His shield undented and untarnished. He went forth to conquer all other temptations, until His final victory and ascension to heaven as Lord of all (see 1 Corinthians 10:13).

The Kingdom Laws

Every kingdom or country has laws and standards by which it exercises authority over its subjects. The kingdom of heaven is no exception. Jesus declared that He came not to destroy the Law but to fulfill it. The old Law was good in its day. Moses and the prophets were far in advance of their time. They were pioneers. Jesus did not destroy this old Law, but He treated it as rudimentary and not as perfect and final.

Jesus says any reform that starts on the outside and works inward is beginning at the wrong place. Christ starts on the inside and works outward. The only way to get a good life is first to get a good heart.

From the lofty pulpit of a mountain, Jesus preached the sermon that contains the laws of His kingdom (Matthew 5–7). Read through these chapters and refresh your memory about this most wonderful of Jesus' discourses. It is filled with lessons to be learned. After more than 1,900 years, this Sermon on the Mount has lost none of its majesty or power, far surpassing any human teaching. The world has not yet caught up with its simple ideals and requirements.

Jesus spoke choice words here to His disciples. The Beatitudes describe the Christian. "Blessed are" begins each one (Matthew 5:3-11). It is not what you are striving to be but what you are in Christ that brings you joy. The Beatitudes provide a picture of Christ. They give a picture of the face of Jesus Himself, not boastingly, but truly describing the perfect Christian.

Even many people who are not Christians claim that the Sermon on the Mount outlines their religion. How little those people understand the depth of the sermon's meaning. It is important that we do not simply praise the rules outlined in the sermon but that we actually practice them in our own lives. If we live by these rules, all our personal relationships will improve, our social wounds will be healed, every dispute between nations will be solved and, yes, the whole world will be a place of order.

The root of these laws is kindness. One day filled with kindness would be a bit of heaven. Love would reign instead of lawlessness. Christ shows us that sin lies, not just in committing the act, but also in the motive behind it (see Matthew 5:21-22,27-28). No one can expect forgiveness who does not forgive (see Matthew 6:12,14-15). Has anyone yet ever fathomed the depth of Matthew 7:12? It is easy to read; it is hard to put into practice.

Jesus preached that the kingdom of heaven is "near" (Matthew 3:2; "at hand," *KJV*); and in the Sermon on the Mount, He sets forth the constitution of the Kingdom—the condition for entrance, its laws, its privileges and rewards. Fourteen times in the sermon, the King says, "I tell you." Mark those 14 times in your Bible. This reveals Jesus' authority as He deals with the law of Moses. People must not only keep the law outwardly but in spirit as well. Notice the effect upon the people: "When Jesus had finished saying these things, the crowds were amazed at his teaching, because he taught as one who had authority, and not as their teachers of the law" (Matthew 7:28-29).

The King's Power

We find the King worked amazing special miracles (Matthew 8–9). He met human needs. There are 12 astonishing miracles in these two chapters. What are they? After Jesus had performed the miracles recorded in chapter 12, "all the people were astonished and said, 'Could this be the Son of David?'" (Matthew 12:23).

The critical teachers of the law now thrust themselves into the scene and pass their hostile judgment on the actions of Jesus (see Matthew 9:3).

The King's Cabinet

Jesus not only preached Himself, but He also gathered others around Him to preach. It was necessary to organize His kingdom in order to reach a wider audience and establish it on a more permanent basis. A king must have subjects who would reflect His light. He told His disciples, "You are the light of the world" (Matthew 5:14).

Jesus still has a great message for the world, and He needs us to carry it. Spiritual ideas are of little value until they are shared by men and women and institutions who will serve as hearts and brains, hands and feet to carry them out. This is what Jesus was doing. He was calling men and women to be His companions so that He could train them to carry on His work.

Where did Jesus find His helpers? Not in the Temple among the doctors and priests and men studying Scripture. He found them on the seashore, mending their nets. Jesus did not call many mighty or noble men but rather "chose the foolish things of the world to shame the wise" (1 Corinthians 1:27).

A list of the disciples is given in Matthew 10:2-4. This is probably the most important catalogue of names in the world. These men were given work to do that would make winning battles and founding empires seem of little consequence in comparison. We find their great message was the kingdom of heaven: "As you go, proclaim this message: 'The kingdom of heaven has come near'" (Matthew 10:7). Their tremendous mission was to start it.

Note some of the warnings and instructions for the disciples Jesus stated in Matthew 10. What were they? If these requirements of discipleship hold true today, could you call yourself a disciple? Read Matthew 10:32-33, and thoughtfully consider Christ's words.

The Kingdom of Heaven

The word "kingdom" occurs more than 55 times in Matthew, for this is the Gospel of the King. The expression "kingdom of heaven" is found more than 30 times here and nowhere else in the Gospels. Most of the 15 parables recorded in Matthew begin with the phrase "The kingdom of heaven is like."

Jewish people understood the phrase "kingdom of heaven." Neither Jesus nor John needed to define it. At Sinai, God said to Israel, "You will be for me a kingdom of priests and a holy nation" (Exodus 19:6). Israel was a theocracy: God was their King; they were His subjects. The prophets had referred to the messianic kingdom again and again.

Read Matthew 13, where Jesus compared the kingdom of heaven to several different things:

- A harvest of wheat separated from weeds
- A mustard seed that grew into a tree
- Yeast worked through the dough
- A treasure hidden in a field
- A pearl of great value
- A net full of fish from which the bad have been thrown away

These parables, often called the secrets of the kingdom of heaven, describe what the result of the presence of the gospel of Christ in the world will be during this present age until the time of His return when He will gather the harvest (see Matthew 13:11; see also Matthew 13:40-43). Initially there will be growth like that of a mustard seed into a tree large enough to let "birds come and perch in its branches" (Matthew 13:32). This is Christendom, which will grow and grow, well beyond its small beginning.

But we see no bright picture of a converted world. Weeds will be mixed with the wheat, good fish will be found with the bad, and there will be yeast in what should be an unleavened loaf. (Yeast, or leaven, is often a symbol of sin. The Spirit never uses yeast as a symbol of anything good. Look this up in your concordance and determine this for yourself.)

Only Christ can determine what is good and what is bad, and at the final harvest, He will divide the two. If we are to have a kingdom on this earth, with the laws that Christ established, then we must have the King. Someday Christ will come in power and great glory and establish His throne on this earth. We will have peace when the Prince of Peace reigns!

Matthew

MATTHEW 16:21–20: REJECTION OF THE KING

The sad story reads that Christ "came to that which was his own, but his own did not receive him" (John 1:11). The gospel of the Kingdom was first preached to those who should have been most prepared, the children of Israel. And although many came to believe in Jesus as the Messiah, the majority of the people rejected their King. From Matthew 12 on we see much controversy among the leaders concerning Jesus.

Jesus announced that the kingdom would be taken away from the Jewish people and given to another nation: "Therefore I tell you that the kingdom of God will be taken away from you and given to a people who will produce its fruit" (Matthew 21:43). The announcement offended the rulers, and "they looked for a way to arrest him" (Matthew 21:46).

Our Lord told Nicodemus the requirement for entrance into the kingdom of heaven (see John 3:3-7). "Whoever" believes may enjoy its privileges and blessings (John 3:16). The kingdom is for the Gentile as well as the Jew.

Why did the Jewish leaders and many of the people refuse the Kingdom? The world today still longs for the golden age; a time of peace is the greatest desire of diplomats and rulers. But they want it in their own way and on their own terms. They want to bring it about by their own efforts. They have no longing for an age brought about by the personal return of the Lord Jesus Christ. It was the same with the people in the day of John the Baptist.

Have you put Christ on the throne of your life? Have you the peace you long for? Have you accepted Christ's terms for your life?

The Church's Universal Call

In Matthew 16, we find Jesus with His disciples in the villiage of Caesarea Philippi. Apparently Jesus wanted to have a private time with His disciples so that He could tell them about something important: His Church.

Only in Matthew's Gospel is the Church named. When the Kingdom was rejected, we find a change in the teachings of Jesus.

He began to talk about the Church instead of the Kingdom (see Matthew 16:18). "Church" comes from the word *ecclesia*, which means "called-out ones." Because all people would not believe in Him, Christ said He was calling out everyone, Jew or Gentile, to belong to His Church, which is His Body. He began to build a new edifice, a new united body of people (see Ephesians 2:14-18).

Life's Most Important Question

When they were far away from the busy scene in which they lived, Jesus asked His disciples, "Who do people say the Son of Man is?" (Matthew 16:13).

This is the important question today! First asked by an obscure Galilean at the foot of Mount Hermon, it has come thundering down through the centuries and has become the mightiest question in the world. What do you think of Christ? What we think determines what we do and are. The ideas we hold about industry, wealth, government, morals and religion mold society and alter lives. So what we think of Christ is the determining force in the world and more than anything else influences our lives and our thoughts.

The disciples gave the answers other people were giving. The answers then were as varied as they are now. All agreed that Jesus was an extraordinary person, at least a prophet or a person who had an element of the supernatural.

Jesus then turned the general question into a sharp personal inquiry. " 'But what about you?' he asked. 'Who do you say I am?' " (Matthew 16:15). Ask yourself this question. Important as the general question is, far more important to each one of us is this personal question. No one can escape it. A neutral answer is impossible. Jesus is either God or an impostor.

Life's Most Important Answer

"You are the Messiah, the Son of the living God!" exclaimed the impulsive, fervent Peter (Matthew 16:16). This answer claims that Christ is the Messiah, the fulfillment of the prophecies of the old Hebrew prophets. This confession is great because it exalts Christ as the Son of God and lifts Him above humanity and crowns Him with deity. From now on He reveals to this handful of disciples new truths about His teachings. After this answer concerning who He was, He said to Peter and the disciples, "On this rock I will build my church" (Matthew 16:18). This is what Christ was going to do—build a Church of which He Himself was to be the chief cornerstone (see Ephesians 2:20). This Church was born on Pentecost (see Acts 2).

For the first time, the fateful shadow of the cross fell across the path of the disciples. From this time on, Jesus drew back the curtain that veiled the future, and He began to show His disciples the things that would happen in the future. He revealed that His path lay toward Jerusalem, where He would face the awful hatred of the priests and Pharisees and then the terrible cross; but He also told them about the glory of His resurrection (see Matthew 16:21).

Jesus did not reveal these things in detail until His disciples were ready to accept them. God often in His mercy hides the future from us.

MATTHEW 21–28: TRIUMPH OF THE KING

On the morning of Palm Sunday, there was a stir in Bethany and along the road leading to Jerusalem. It was understood that Jesus was to enter the city that day. Crowds of people were gathering. A colt was procured; and the disciples, having thrown their robes over it, placed Jesus upon it, and the procession started. This little parade could not compare in magnificence with any procession at the coronation of a king or the inauguration of a president; but it meant much more for the world. Jesus for the first time permitted a public recognition and celebration of His rights as Messiah-King. The end was approaching with awful swiftness, and He must offer Himself as the Messiah, even if only to be rejected.

In their enthusiasm, the people tore off branches from the palm and olive trees and carpeted the highway, while shouts rang through the air. They believed in Jesus, and their warm enthusiasm reflected their pride in their King. In answer to the crowds who asked, "Who is this?" they boldly answered, "This is Jesus, the prophet from Nazareth of Galilee" (Matthew 21:10-11). It took courage to say that in Jerusalem. Jesus was not entering the city as a triumphant conqueror as the Romans had done. No sword was in His hand. Over Him floated no bloodstained banner. His mission was salvation!

OLD TESTAMENT PROMISE AND NEW TESTAMENT FULFILLMENT

> Roaring lions tearing their prey open their mouths wide
> against me . . . a band of evil men has encircled me, they have pierced
> my hands and my feet . . . people stare and gloat over me.
>
> PSALM 22:13,16-17

> Two robbers were crucified with him, one on his right
> and one on his left. Those who passed by hurled insults at him,
> shaking their heads and saying, "You who are going to destroy the
> temple and build it in three days, save yourself! Come down
> from the cross, if you are the Son of God!"
>
> MATTHEW 27:38-40

Christ's authority was brought into question as He went into the Temple and ordered the merchants out, overturning their tables and telling them that they had made the house of God a den of thieves (see Matthew 21:12-13). A bitter controversy followed. "Then the Pharisees went out and laid plans to trap him in his words" (Matthew 22:15).

In the evening the crowds dispersed, and Jesus quietly returned to Bethany. Apparently nothing in the way of making Jesus King had been accomplished. His hour had not yet come.

Matthew

Christ must be Savior first; then He would come again as King of kings and Lord of lords.

The Future of the Kingdom

When Jesus delivered His Mount Olivet discourse, He foretold the condition of the world after His ascension until He comes back in glory to judge the nations, according to their treatment of "brothers and sisters of mine," the Jewish people (Matthew 25:40). This is not the judgment of the "great white throne," which is the judgment of the wicked dead (Revelation 20:11). Neither is it the judgment seat of Christ, which is the judgment of saints according to their works (see 2 Corinthians 5:10). It is the judgment of Gentile nations concerning their attitude toward God's people.

Much of Jesus' discourse in Matthew 24 and 25 is devoted to Christ's second coming. He exhorts us to be ready in the parables of the faithful servant (see Matthew 24:45-51), the 10 virgins (see Matthew 25:1-13) and the talents (see Matthew 25:14-30).

The Death and Resurrection of the King

Up until this point, we have learned about some of the highlights in the life of Jesus; now we step into the shadows as we enter Gethsemane. We see the Son of Abraham, the sacrifice, dying so that all the nations of the earth will be blessed by Him. Jesus was slain because He was named "the King of Israel" (Matthew 27:42). He was raised from the dead because He was the King of all (see Acts 2:30-36). Although a large number of disciples believed in Jesus and followed Him, the opposition of the religious leaders was bitter and they determined to put Him to death. On the grounds of blasphemy and of claiming to be the King of the Jews (the latter making Himself the enemy of the Roman emperor), Jesus was condemned by Pilate to be crucified.

Matthew is not alone in his record of the terrible circumstances of the Savior's last hours; but he makes us feel as if the mock regal trappings—the crown of thorns, the sceptre, the title over the cross—are evidence, though their purpose was only to scorn, of the kingly claim.

After hanging on the cross for six hours, the Savior died—not from physical suffering alone but also of a broken heart, for He bore the sins of the whole world to become the world's Redeemer!

OLD TESTAMENT PROMISE AND NEW TESTAMENT FULFILLMENT

This is how you are to eat it: with your cloak tucked into your belt, your sandals on your feet and your staff in your hand. Eat it in haste; it is the Lord's Passover. On that same night I will pass through Egypt and strike down every firstborn—both men and animals—and I will bring judgment on all the gods of Egypt. I am the Lord. The blood will be a sign for you on the houses where you are; and when I see the blood, I will pass over you. No destructive plague will touch you when I strike Egypt. This is a day you are to commemorate; for the generations to come you shall celebrate it as a festival to the Lord—a lasting ordinance.

EXODUS 12:11-14

Take and eat; this is my body. . . . Drink from it, all of you. This is my blood of the covenant, which is poured out for many for the forgiveness of sins.

MATTHEW 26:26-28

For Christ, our Passover lamb, has been sacrificed.

1 CORINTHIANS 5:7

The Great Price of Redemption

Jesus was put in Joseph's tomb, and on the third day He rose, as He had said He would. This is the supreme test of His kingship. People thought He was dead and His kingdom had failed. But by His resurrection, Christ assured His disciples that the King still lived and that one day He will come back to establish His kingdom on earth.

The ascension of Jesus is not recorded in Matthew. The curtain falls with the Messiah still on earth, for it is on earth that the Son of David is yet to reign in glory. The last time the Jews saw Christ, He was on the Mount of Olives. The next time they see Him, He will again be on the Mount of Olives (see Zechariah 14:4; Acts 1:11).

The Commission for All Disciples

Matthew closes his Gospel with Jesus' climactic announcement of His great commission: "All authority in heaven and on earth has been given to me. Therefore go and make disciples of all nations, baptizing them in the name of the Father and of the Son and of the Holy Spirit, and teaching them to obey everything I have commanded you. And surely I am with you always, to the very end of the age" (Matthew 28:18-20).

On what mission were they sent? To overrun the world with armies and use weapons to force people to submit to them? No, they were to "make disciples of all nations."

From the mountaintop of Jesus' ascension, Jesus' disciples began this mission, radiating from that center out into the world; and Jesus' disciples will continue "to make disciples" until they have reached everywhere in the world. Christian faith is not a national or racial religion, and it has no natural boundaries. It is meant to reach around the globe.

3

Understanding Mark

Mark Portrays Jesus Christ, the Servant of God

SELECTED BIBLE READINGS

D A Y O F T H E W E E K	Sunday: Mark 1:1-20	The Servant's Coming and Testing
	Monday: Mark 2–3:25	The Servant's Works
	Tuesday: Mark 4–6:13	The Servant's Words
	Wednesday: Mark 6:32–8:26	The Servant's Miracles
	Thursday: Mark 8:27–10:34	The Servant's Revelation
	Friday: Mark 11–12	The Servant's Rejection
	Saturday: Mark 14–16	The Servant's Death and Triumph

(M A I N   T O P I C)

AUTHOR: Although the Gospel of Mark does not name its author, a tradition dating from the second century ascribes this book to John Mark (see Acts 12:12), a companion and spiritual son of Peter (see 1 Peter 5:13), and also an associate of Paul and Barnabas in their missionary endeavors. The early Church fathers also unanimously testified that the apostle Mark was the author.

DATE: The Gospel of Mark was likely one of the first books written in the New Testament, possibly in the late 50s or early 60s AD.

PURPOSE AND SUMMARY: Scholars generally agree that Mark wrote his Gospel in Rome for the Gentile believers. Mark accounts for the ministry of Jesus from His baptism to His ascension into heaven. Most scholars agree that Mark's purpose was neither biographical nor historical but theological: to present Jesus as the Christ, the mighty worker rather than the great teacher. Hence, Mark makes fewer references to the parables and discourses of Jesus, but he meticulously records each of Jesus' healings and miracles—20 specific miracles and allusions to others—as evidence of the fact that Jesus was the Messiah sent from God.

John, whose surname was Mark, is the author of the Gospel of Mark (see Acts 12:12,25). He was the son of Mary and cousin of Barnabas (see Colossians 4:10), and he likely was a native of Jerusalem. It is believed that the Upper Room of Mark's mother's house in Jerusalem is where the disciples met. He accompanied Paul and Barnabas to Antioch and was the cause of a serious disagreement between them (see Acts 12:25; 13:5). Then he left them, probably on account of hardships (see Acts 13:13). Finally he became a great help to Paul (see Colossians 4:10-11; 2 Timothy 4:11). Peter was the means of Mark's conversion and affectionately speaks of him as "my son" (1 Peter 5:13). We see the influence of Peter's teaching in this Gospel.

If we turn to Mark 10:45, we can quite easily determine Mark's object in writing his Gospel: "For even the Son of Man did not come to be served, but to serve, and to give his life as a ransom for many." Unlike Matthew, Mark was not trying to prove certain statements and prophecies concerning Jesus. His only object in writing was to tell clearly certain facts about Jesus—His deeds more than His words. That Jesus is the Son of God he proves, not by declaring how He came to earth, but by showing what He accomplished during His brief life on this earth, how His coming changed the world.

There is a general agreement that Mark's Gospel was written for Roman readers. The Roman culture differed from the Jewish culture in many ways. The Romans highly valued common sense. Their religion had to be practical. They had no interest in tracing beliefs back into the past. Legal genealogies and fulfillments of prophecy would leave them cold. Arguing fine points of Scripture interpretation held no interest for them. They might have said, "I know nothing of your Scriptures and care nothing for your peculiar notions; but I would be glad to hear a plain story of the life this man Jesus lived. Tell me what He did. Let me see Him just as He was."

The Gospel of Mark differs widely from Matthew in length, character and scope. Matthew has 28 chapters, abounds in parables and portrays Christ as the Son of David with kingly dignity and authority (see Matthew 28:18). Mark has 16 chapters (it is the shortest Gospel), relates only four parables and portrays Christ as the humble but perfect servant of Jehovah. Angels minister to Him.

GENERAL CHARACTERISTICS OF MARK'S GOSPEL

The skill of a gifted artist may lie in what he or she leaves out. An amateur crowds everything in. In keeping with Mark's central purpose of emphasizing Jesus as the servant, many points covered in Matthew are omitted in Mark:

- There is nothing about the virgin birth. No reference to Jesus' birth is made in the whole Gospel. This is significant. No one is interested in the pedigree of a servant.

- There is no visit of wise men. A servant does not receive homage.

- No account of Jesus as the boy in the Temple is given. During Mark's day (as it is today) people demanded a Christ who can do things. They were not interested in Jesus the boy but Christ the man who was able and willing to accomplish things.

- There is no Sermon on the Mount. Matthew devoted three whole chapters to this sermon, but Mark presents Christ as a perfect workman; such a servant has no kingdom and frames no laws.

- No quotations from the prophets are recalled. Mark's one direct quotation from the prophets is found in Mark 1:2. Matthew quotes the prophets on every page.

- No divine titles are used. Jesus is never called a king in Mark, except in derision. Matthew says, " 'They will call him Immanuel' (which means 'God with us')" (Matthew 1:23). Not so in Mark. Mark calls Him "Teacher" ("Master," *KJV*). Other evangelists call Him "Lord." Matthew 8:25 says, "Lord, save us! We're going to drown!" Mark 4:38 says, "Teacher, don't you care if we drown?"

- Matthew records 14 parables; Mark only four—the sower, the seed growing secretly (peculiar to Mark), the mustard seed and the wicked husbandmen.

- Miracles have a leading place in Mark, as parables have in Matthew. A servant works; a king speaks. Twenty miracles are detailed in Mark.

- There is no statement that Jesus' work was finished at His death. In John 19:30, Jesus said, "It is finished." This is not found in Mark. It is not for a servant to say when his work is done.

- There is no introduction in Mark. The other Gospels have lengthy openings, but the opening verse in Mark simply says, "The beginning of the good news about Jesus the Messiah," and then Mark adds, "Son of God," to guard His divine glory. How different this is from Matthew, where the focus is the King.

The word "gospel" is used eight times in Matthew, Mark, Luke and John together, and five of those times are in Mark. Yes, the servant is to bear good news! Another term that predominates Mark is the Greek word *eutheos*, which is translated as "immediately," "at once," "as soon as" and "without delay." In all, this expression is found no fewer than 20 times in Mark's Gospel. This is a servant's word.

In the *King James Version*, 12 out of 16 chapters in Mark open with the little word "and." Jesus' service was one complete, perfect whole, with no pause or breaks in it; it was continuous. We may slack off but not our Lord.

OLD TESTAMENT PROMISE AND
NEW TESTAMENT FULFILLMENT

A voice of one calling: "In the desert prepare the way for the Lord; make straight in the wilderness a highway for our God."

ISAIAH 40:3

And this was his [John the Baptist's] message: "After me will come one more powerful than I, the thongs of whose sandals I am not worthy to stoop down and untie. I baptize you with water, but he will baptize you with the Holy Spirit.

MARK 1:7-8

MARK 1:1-13: THE SERVANT PREPARED

The book of Mark skips over the first 30 years of Jesus' life, but these years were all needed for His human preparation for His life's work. Jesus must have grown to sympathize with a human's daily toil. Surely, He wrestled, like Jacob, with life's problems and fought many battles in the arena of His heart. Certainly, He meditated on the needs of His nation until His mental anguish almost consumed Him.

Preparation in life is always needed. Jesus' life illustrated this. The foundations of a lighthouse are necessary, though they are unseen beneath the surface. A plant sends its roots into the dark soil before it can bring forth a flower and leaf. Look at the 40 years Moses spent in the desert before he started his great work; the long period Elijah spent before he appeared before King Ahab; the early years Amos spent on a farm; the 30 years of training that John the Baptist went through. So it was with Jesus! He spent 30 years in obscurity in Nazareth before He appeared for three years of public ministry.

Getting ready for our life's work is of tremendous importance. Don't become impatient if Christ uses time to prepare you for life.

Preparation by a Messenger

This Gospel begins with John the Baptist making people ready for the coming of the Messiah. John's coming was in fulfillment of a messianic prophecy: "I will send my messenger ahead of you, who will prepare your way" (Mark 1:2). This quotation refers to Malachi 3:1 and Isaiah 40:3. In Isaiah, the messenger is known simply as "a voice": "A voice of one calling: 'In the wilderness prepare the way for the LORD; make straight in the desert a highway for our God'" (Isaiah 40:3). It is this "voice" that was to announce Jesus Christ.

We see this strange man appear on the scene in an almost sensational way: "John wore clothing made of camel's hair, with a leather belt around his waist, and he ate locusts and wild honey" (Mark 1:6).

There is a lesson here for us. God does not always choose the kind of person we would select. He often picks "the foolish things of the world to shame the wise . . . the weak things of the world to shame the strong" (1 Corinthians 1:27). No doubt, if we were to select someone to announce Christ's arrival, we would choose someone of superior birth, well educated, with a sterling reputation. This person would have to be eloquent and a fearless champion of great causes. Not so with God. Of humble birth, probably only slightly educated, not well known, and dressed like a desert hermit, John the Baptist was approved by God (see Matthew 11:11).

John's message was as startling as his appearance: "Prepare the way for the Lord, make straight paths for him" (Mark 1:3). A true revival is always a revival of righteousness.

Preparation by Baptism

John and Jesus met one day. John recognized immediately that this Man was not someone who needed the baptism of repentance that he was preaching. There was in this face a purity and majesty that struck John's heart with a sense of his own unworthiness. This man was the Son of God. John hesitated before he said, "I need to be baptized by you, and do you come to me?" (Matthew 3:14).

Jesus was, however, baptized with John's baptism in order to obey a divine order: "Let it be so now; it is proper for us to do this to fulfill all righteousness" (Matthew 3:15). Jesus set a seal of approval on John's message and work, and acknowledged him as His own true forerunner. The baptism by John was ordered by God and therefore was necessary for all those who acknowledged God and meant to keep His commandments.

Because Christ was the standard for and an example of righteousness, He would fulfill every duty that He required of others, including being baptized (see 1 Corinthians 10:13).

Preparation by Receiving the Holy Spirit

"Just as Jesus was coming up out of the water, he saw heaven being torn open and the Spirit descending on him like a dove" (Mark 1:10). The Spirit descended, not only in the manner of a dove, but also in the bodily shape of a dove (see Luke 3:22). This was a symbol; the coming of the Spirit Himself was a reality. In any service for God, the Spirit always aids the preparation by giving power and equipment. He is God's great agent for spiritual warfare.

Because Jesus went down into the baptismal water of obedience to God, He came up under an opened sky with the Holy Spirit descending upon Him; and He could hear the voice of His Father, declaring Him to be His beloved Son.

Jesus came up out of that water a new man into a new world. His relationship to His Father and His mission were proclaimed.

Preparation by a Divine Call

"A voice came from heaven" (Mark 1:11). God endorsed Jesus and His mission, and showed to the Jewish nation that Jesus was the Messiah: "God anointed Jesus of Nazareth with the Holy Spirit and power, and . . . he went around doing good and healing all who were under the power of the devil, because God was with him" (Acts 10:38). Mark 1:11 has been called Mark's Gospel in a nutshell. Later we hear this same voice at the Transfiguration: "This is my Son, whom I love. Listen to him!" (Mark 9:7).

OLD TESTAMENT PROMISE AND NEW TESTAMENT FULFILLMENT

> I will proclaim the decree of the Lord: He said to me, "You are my Son; today I have become your Father. Ask of me, and I will make the nations your inheritance, the ends of the earth your possession."

PSALM 2:7-8

> Then a cloud appeared and enveloped them, and a voice came from the cloud: "This is my Son, whom I love. Listen to him!"

MARK 9:7

Preparation by Testing

Baptism and temptation are here crowded together. Hardly had the voice from heaven died away then we hear a whisper from hell. Out of the baptismal benediction of the Father, Jesus stepped into a desperate struggle with the devil.

Mark says, "At once the Spirit sent him out into the wilderness," which shows how quickly the Spirit moves (Mark 1:12). "At once" indicates continuity, showing that temptation was as much a part of the preparation of the servant for His work as His baptism. Suffering and trials are as much God's plan as thrills and triumphs. Jesus was "sent" to be tempted. It was no accident or evil fate but a divine appointment.

Temptation has its place in this world. We could never develop without it. There is nothing wrong in being tempted. The wrong begins when we consent to it. We are not to run into temptation of our own accord. Jesus did not go by His own choice but was sent by the Spirit. We will find that the path of duty often takes us through temptations, but "no temptation has overtaken you except what is common to mankind. And God is faithful; he will not let you be tempted beyond what you can bear. But when you are tempted, he will also provide a way out so that you can endure it" (1 Corinthians 10:13). He always makes a way of escape! This subject is of great importance. Be sure you understand it.

MARK 1:14–8:30—THE SERVANT WORKING

As mentioned earlier, there is a continuous, unbroken service of the servant recorded in this Gospel. We read, "And He did this. And He said that." He must teach people; they were in darkness. He must cheer people; they were without hope. He must heal people; they were sick and suffering. He must free people; they were under the power of Satan. He must pardon and cleanse people; they were sinful.

We see Jesus preaching by the seashore and selecting four of the fishermen to become His first disciples to learn under His guidance how to become "fishers of men" (Mark 1:26, *KJV*). Who were they? Read Mark 1:16-20. They were to take all their practical knowledge and skill used to catch fish and use them to catch men and women. Which disciple was called in Mark 2?

It is interesting to note that Jesus never called any idle person. He called busy and successful people to follow Him. Any business can be adapted to be used in service for Christ. How was Christ's call received? "At once they left their nets and followed him" (Mark 1:18). Too often there is time lost between our call and our coming; our doing lags far behind our duty.

The action in Mark is rapid, and events appear to be happening before our very eyes. Mark's descriptions are short and direct, but he preserves many things for us that would otherwise have been lost. It is only in the Gospel of Mark that we are told, for example, that Jesus was a carpenter (see Mark 6:3).

Mark

Mark tells us that Jesus took little children "in his arms" (Mark 9:36; 10:16). Mark tells us that Jesus was "grieved" (Mark 3:5, *KJV*); that He "sighed" (Mark 8:12). He "wondered" (Mark 6:51, *KJV*). He "loved" (Mark 10:21).

The Servant Observes Sabbath

Let us spend with Jesus the Sabbath that is recorded in Mark 1:21-34, going with Him to synagogue, listening to His preaching, watching Him when interrupted by a maniac, casting out the unclean spirit and making the healing a powerful aid to His teaching. Then, after service, let us go with Him to Peter's house and see Him heal Peter's wife's mother of a severe fever; and then let us spend the Sabbath afternoon in quiet rest and friendly conversation.

Toward evening we will look out in the beautiful twilight and see men and women coming toward the house, bringing great numbers of people, sick with every kind of disease, and watch them as Jesus lays His tender hands on them and heals them. The lame jump from their stretchers and leap for joy; the blind open their eyes and see their healer; faces lined by suffering suddenly express unbelievable happiness as painful diseases are cured.

Mark records a wonderful statement concerning the Sabbath: "The Sabbath was made for man, not man for the Sabbath" (Mark 2:27). This great saying by Jesus is the central principle of Sabbath observance. The Sabbath is not made to annoy humankind, to confine them, to impoverish them, but to enrich and bless them! Try spending one Lord's day as Jesus did. I believe you will like it, and the Lord will be pleased.

Christ answers a question about what is proper to do on the Sabbath with a practical illustration (see Mark 3:1-5). His conclusion is that whatever deed is really helpful to people is proper for the Sabbath and is in perfect accord with what God meant the day to be. He illustrated this truth with this miracle of healing. Seven of Jesus' recorded miracles were performed on the Sabbath. The Sabbath was "made." It is God's gift to people.

Mark

The Servant Heals

In Mark, Jesus appears at once as one "anointed . . . with power" and as fully engaged in His work (Acts 10:38). You will find no long discussions in these next chapters, but you will find many mighty deeds. Demons were cast out (see Mark 1:21-28); fever banished (see Mark 1:29-31); different diseases healed (see Mark 1:32-34); lepers made whole (see Mark 1:40-45); a paralytic man made to walk (see Mark 2:1-12); a withered hand cured (see Mark 3:1-5); multitudes healed (see Mark 3:6-12); storm at sea quelled (see Mark 4:35-41); maniac's mind restored (see Mark 5:1-15); woman's hemorrhage stopped (see Mark 5:21-34); Jairus's daughter brought back to life (see Mark 5:35-43); five thousand fed (see Mark 6:32-44); the sea made into His sidewalk (see Mark 6:45-51); all that touched Him were made whole (see Mark 6:53-56); the deaf heard and the dumb spoke (see Mark 7:31-37); four thousand fed (see Mark 8:1-9); a blind man healed (see Mark 8:22-26).

The miracles of Jesus were proof of His mission from God. They showed that He was the promised Redeemer and King, the One we all need. Because Jesus was God, miracles were as natural to Him as acts of will are to us! Through His miracles, Jesus inspired faith in many of those who saw and heard Him.

The servant is always found working: "As long as it is day, we must do the works of him who sent me. Night is coming, when no one can work" (John 9:4). This brief description of our Lord's ministry shows how full His days were. How empty our own lives seem in comparison!

The Servant Prays

The morning following the great Sabbath day of preaching and healing, Jesus rose very early and went out of the city to a lonely place and prayed (see Mark 1:35). His work was growing rapidly, and Jesus needed communion with heaven, an intimate conversation with God. It seems as if during His prayer He was told to do a larger work, for He soon leaves on His first Galilean tour of healing and preaching (see Mark 1:37-39). Only one healing event of this tour, which lasted several days, is recorded—that of a leper whose disease was incurable (see Mark 1:40-45).

If the Son of God needed to pray before He undertook His work, how much more should we pray. Perhaps if we lack success in life, it is because we fail to pray. In other words, we have not because we ask not (see James 4:2).

The Servant Forgives Sin

"A few days later . . . the people heard that he had come home" (Mark 2:1). It is remarkable how rapidly news spread in Jesus' time, without newspapers, television, phones or the Internet. But in another part of the city, a paralytic man and his friends had heard of this new servant and His gospel of healing. His four friends brought him to Jesus and let him down into the presence of the teacher. We find in this healing the test and proof of Jesus' power, not only as a healer of the body, but also as a healer of the soul. "Who can forgive sins but God alone?" (Mark 2:7), the people said. Sins are against God and, therefore, He only can forgive. Jesus said, " 'But I want you to know that the Son of Man has authority on earth to forgive sins.' So he said to the man, 'I tell you, get up, take your mat and go home' " (Mark 2:10-11).

Through this miracle, God endorsed Jesus' claim to be the Messiah. The man got up, took up his mat and, in front of everyone, walked as a living witness to Jesus' power over sin, a visible illustration of the work Jesus came to do. Jesus came to give His life as a ransom for many so that people's sins would be forgiven: "All have sinned," and all need a Savior (Romans 3:23).

The Servant Teaches

We find the account of choosing the 12 apostles in Mark 3:13-21. Notice the fourteenth verse; it tells why Jesus chose these men: "that they might be with him." Mark it in your Bible. This is what Jesus wants of His disciples today—that they will take time to be in His presence and communicate with Him. In John 15:15, He says, "I no longer call you servants. . . . I have called you friends."

OLD TESTAMENT PROMISE AND
NEW TESTAMENT FULFILLMENT

The stone the builders rejected has become the capstone; the Lord
has done this, and it is marvelous in our eyes.

PSALM 118:22-23

The stone the builders rejected has become the capstone; the Lord has
done this, and it is marvelous in our eyes. Then they looked for a way
to arrest him because they knew he had spoken the parable against them.

MARK 12:10-12

As you turn to Mark 4, notice once again that the opening
word is "And" (*KJV*). "And he began again to teach" (*KJV*) as on for-
mer occasions (see Mark 4:1). What a wonderful teacher is Jesus!

Everyone should master the parables of the Kingdom in Mark
4. They were a special teaching technique used by Christ. Jesus used
this method of instruction because of the growing hostility to Him
and His message. He was surrounded by enemies who tried to find
fault with what He had to say, but no one could object to a simple
story. Besides, stories are easy to remember by almost everyone.

A parable is an analogy. It assumes a likeness between heavenly
and earthly things. "Parable" comes from the Greek word meaning
"beside" and "to throw." A parable, then, is a form of teaching in
which one thing is thrown beside another to make a comparison.

The parable of the sower, for example, is actually about the
obstacles that people have to accepting and understanding the
Gospel (see Mark 4:3-20). Besides the parable of the sower, our
Lord told other parables as recorded by Mark in this chapter:

- The parable of the lamp—Mark 4:21-25
- The parable of the sprouting seed—Mark 4:26-29
- The parable of the mustard seed—Mark 4:30-33

After interpreting the parables, Jesus took a boat to cross the Sea of Galilee to escape the crowd. On the way, as the weary servant fell asleep, a violent storm came up on the Sea of Galilee. About to perish, the frantic disciples woke up Jesus. At a word from His lips, the sea became calm. He had power over the elements (see Mark 4:35-41).

The Servant Tests the People

Mark 5 begins again with "and" (*KJV*). Jesus is still working. What does He do now? Read parallel accounts in Matthew 8:28-34; Luke 8:26-39. Compare this miracle with other recorded cures of people possessed by demons (see Matthew 9:32-33; Mark 1:23-26; Matthew 17:14-18; Luke 9:38-42).

The miracle recorded in Mark 5, like all others, tested the character of people. It surprised them and disclosed their true natures. Notice the contrast in the way people receive the work of Christ.

Some shunned the Savior: "Those tending the pigs ran off" (Mark 5:14). Others "were afraid" and "pleaded with him to leave their region" (Mark 5:15,17). Doubtless there were other herds of swine, and they feared the loss of them. What a true picture of the attitude of many toward Christ! There is some sort of lucrative business that each does not want to give up. There are some sins that lie close to their hearts. For these reasons people push Christ away.

Some seek the Savior. The healed man "begged to go with him" (Mark 5:18). It is the same with people today. People either ask Jesus to "leave," because they want to keep their sins, or they ask Him to remain "with" them because they want to lose their sins. Do you want to keep or lose your sin?

The Servant Sends the Disciples

Jesus started out on a third preaching tour of Galilee (see Mark 6). He sent forth the 12 disciples, two by two, on independent missions (see Mark 6:7-13). Matthew 10 records the instructions they received. As they preached, Herod heard about them, and we read about his uneasy conscience, thinking that the man he had murdered was back to haunt him (see Mark 6:14-29). How much people recklessly give away in order to enjoy fleeting pleasures. For a glass of wine, a moment of passion, a little more money, a position of honor, they give away half—no, *all*—the kingdom of their souls. Gone are their health, homes, friendships, peace, happiness and eternal lives. Like Esau, they sell their birthright for a bit of stew. Like Judas, they sell their Savior for 30 bits of metal.

After the apostles were trained, Jesus sent them out on an extensive missionary tour among the villages of Galilee (see Mark 6:12-13). On returning they "gathered around Jesus" (Mark 6:30), probably at their regular rendezvous, Capernaum. They reported on their sermons, the number of conversions and the miracles that they had performed. No Christian work can be carried on for any length of time without frequent talks with Christ. We need His sympathy, approval, guidance and strength.

OLD TESTAMENT PROMISE AND NEW TESTAMENT FULFILLMENT

Rejoice greatly, O Daughter of Zion! Shout, Daughter of Jerusalem! See, your king comes to you, righteous and having salvation, gentle and riding on a donkey, on a colt, the foal of a donkey.

ZECHARIAH 9:9

When they brought the colt to Jesus and threw their cloaks over it, he sat on it. Those who went ahead and those who followed shouted, "Hosanna!" "Blessed is he who comes in the name of the Lord!"

MARK 11:7,9

MARK 8:31–15—THE SERVANT REJECTED

Even before Mark sets forth Christ's direct claim to be King of the kingdom, he reveals the way the King is to be received. Jesus said, "The Son of Man must suffer many things" (Mark 8:31):

- He is to be rejected by the elders, chief priests and scribes (see Mark 8:31).
- He is to be delivered by treachery (see Mark 9:31).
- He is to be put to death by the Romans (see Mark 10:32-45).
- He is to rise again the third day (see Mark 9:31).

Jesus claimed the kingdom by presenting Himself as the heir of David (according to the prophecy of Zechariah 9:9) when He arrived in Jerusalem (see Mark 11:1-11).

How did the people accept this King? At first they welcomed Him because they hoped He would free them from servitude to Rome and from the poverty they endured. But when He entered the Temple and showed that His mission was a spiritual one, He was hated by the religious leaders with a satanic hatred that led to the plot to put Him to death (see Mark 14:1).

OLD TESTAMENT PROMISE AND NEW TESTAMENT FULFILLMENT

For my house will be called a house of prayer for all nations.

ISAIAH 56:7

On reaching Jerusalem, Jesus entered the temple area and began driving out those who were buying and selling there. And as he taught them, he said, "Is it not written: 'My house will be called a house of prayer for all nations?' But you have made it 'a den of robbers.'"

MARK 11:15,17

The Last Conflict

After Christ's public ministry, described in Mark 10:46–11:26, we read of His last conflict with the Jewish authorities and of His triumph over the leaders (see Mark 11:27–12:12).

Jesus sought to persuade the Jews to receive Him as the Messiah (see Mark 11:15–12:36). It was a busy Tuesday. Jesus was occupied from morning till night in one great and powerful effort to induce the Jewish nation to acknowledge Him and thus become that glorious nation for which it had been set apart to bless the world.

In the beautiful Temple courts, the simple Galilean met the religious authorities, arrayed in all the pomp of their official regalia. There are four sharp controversies:

1. The scribes and chief priests ask Him, "By what authority are you doing these things? . . . And who gave you authority to do this?" (Mark 11:28).

2. The Pharisees and Herodians try to catch Him in His words and ask, "Is it right to pay the imperial tax?" (Mark 12:14).

3. The Sadducees, who say there is no resurrection, ask Him, "At the resurrection whose wife will she be, since the seven were married to her?" (Mark 12:23).

4. The scribes ask Him, "Of all the commandments, which is the most important?" (Mark 12:28).

After Jesus answered them all, "from then on no one dared ask him any more questions" (Mark 12:34).

It would seem that by answering the questions, Jesus could not escape being treasonous to the Roman government, but He came away untouched. Hour by hour Jesus met the attacks, and He silenced His enemies, but they still refused to believe Him. Then He exposed all their hypocritical practices in words that fell like bombs. He tried to break through their walls of prejudice and get them to repent before it was too late, but all seemed to be in vain.

Before He goes to the cross, Jesus reveals the future to His troubled disciples (see the Olivet discourse, Mark 13). He tells them about the end of this age and about the great tribulation, and He ends with the promise of His return in power and glory.

The scheming of the chief priests to put Jesus to death, and the anointing of His body in preparation for burial, opens chapter 14 (see verse 8). Then the sad story of His betrayal at the hand of His own disciple, the celebration of the Passover and the institution of the Lord's Supper all are crowded into 25 short verses. Adding insult to injury is Peter's denial of his Lord (see Mark 14:10-11,26-31,66-71).

Then Mark records how the sufferings of Jesus in Gethsemane and on Calvary fulfilled the prophecies of Isaiah and Isaiah's great message that the Son of God would become the servant of God in order to redeem the world (see Isaiah 53).

OLD TESTAMENT PROMISE AND NEW TESTAMENT FULFILLMENT

We all, like sheep, have gone astray, each of us has turned to his own way; and the Lord has laid on him the iniquity of us all.

ISAIAH 53:6

For Christ died for sins once for all, the righteous for the unrighteous, to bring you to God. He was put to death in the body but made alive by the Spirit

1 PETER 3:18

MARK 16: THE SERVANT EXALTED

After the servant had given His life as a ransom for many, He rose from the dead. Compare the two versions of the Great Commission (see Mark 16:15; see also Matthew 28:19-20). In Mark we do not hear a King say, "All authority in heaven and on earth has been given to me," as in Matthew (Matthew 28:18). In Mark we see in Jesus' words that His disciples are to take His place, and He will serve in and through them. He is still the servant, though risen (see Mark 16:20). The command for service resounds with urgency. Not a corner of the world is to be left unvisited, not a soul to be left out!

Finally Jesus was received into heaven to sit at the right hand of God (see Mark 16:19). He who had taken on Himself the form of a servant is now highly exalted (see Philippians 2:7-9). He is in the place of power, always interceding for us. He is our Advocate.

But Christ is with us. The servant is always working in us and through us. We are laborers together with Him (see 1 Corinthians 3:9). He is still working with us (see Mark 16:20). Let us, being redeemed, follow our model and go forth to serve also! "Therefore, my dear brothers and sisters, stand firm. Let nothing move you. Always give yourselves fully to the work of the Lord, because you know that your labor in the Lord is not in vain" (1 Corinthians 15:58).

POINTS TO REMEMBER

All the way through, the perfect servant of God was dogged by His enemies. The enemy is not dead! God's servants today are called to tread a similar path.

Feeding the five thousand is one of the most important miracles performed by Jesus (see Mark 6:30-44). Evidently it made a special impression on the writers of the Gospels, as it is the only one of the 35 miracles that is recorded by all four. Review this miracle carefully. Notice that Jesus served in an orderly way.

Jesus was sold for 30 pieces of silver, the price of a slave. He was executed as only slaves were! Yes, Christ was the suffering servant and died for me! He bore my sins in His own body on the tree.

No reference is made by Mark that in the garden of Gethsemane, Jesus had the right to summon 12 legions of angels if He wanted to. No promise of the Kingdom is given to the dying thief on the cross. These claims are made by a king (in Matthew), but they are not mentioned by a servant.

OLD TESTAMENT PROMISE AND NEW TESTAMENT FULFILLMENT

The Lord says to my Lord: "Sit at my right hand until I make your enemies a footstool for your feet" (Ps. 110:1).

PSALM 110:1

After the Lord Jesus had spoken to them, he was taken up into heaven and he sat at the right hand of God.

MARK 16:19

A Confession of Faith

Peter's confession of faith should be on everyone's lips (see Mark 8:29). Jesus did not tell His disciples who He was. He waited for them to tell Him. When He asked, "Who do you say I am?" the climax of His ministry was reached. He was testing the chosen 12 to determine whether His teaching had been effective. Peter's answer gave Him the assurance that His goal had been attained.

What did the Pharisees think of Jesus? They had agreed to put Him to death.

What did the multitude think of Him? They deserted Him.

What did the disciples think of Him? Peter gave the answer.

What do you think of Christ?

The Greatest Sin

The greatest sin of this age, as of every age, is the rejection of Jesus Christ. Everyone who has heard the gospel must either accept the Lord as Savior or reject Him. The people of Jesus' day made their choice, and the people of our day must make theirs.

The wonderful servant who shines in the Gospels—this vision of God in the flesh—are you to look and then pass by as though you had only seen a work of art? This voice that has continued to speak throughout the centuries, are you to listen as though it were just the voice of a gifted speaker? What is Jesus to you? A name or your master? If you cannot answer the question as Peter did, will you sign this covenant:

> I promise to examine carefully the evidence that the Bible is God's book and that Jesus Christ is God's Son and man's Savior; and if I find reason to believe that this book is true and He is man's Savior, I will accept Him, confess Him before men and follow Him.

_____

(Signed)

Mark

Understanding Luke

Luke Portrays Jesus Christ, the Son of Man

 SELECTED BIBLE READINGS

DAY OF THE WEEK		MAIN TOPIC
Sunday: Luke 1–3	The Man Made Like His Brothers	
Monday: Luke 4–8:3	The Man Tempted as We Are	
Tuesday: Luke 8:4–12:48	The Man Able to Sympathize	
Wednesday: Luke 12:49–16	The Man Going About His Father's Business	
Thursday: Luke 17–19:27	The Man Whose Speech Is Unique	
Friday: Luke 19:28–23	The Man Who Is Our Kinsman-Redeemer	
Saturday: Luke 24	The Man Who Showed Resurrection Glory	

AUTHOR: The Gospel of Luke does not identify its author, but it is clear that the same author wrote both Luke and Acts, addressing both to Theophilus, possibly a Roman dignitary (see Luke 1:3; Acts 1:1). The tradition from the earliest days of the Church has been that Luke, a physician and a close companion of the apostle Paul, wrote both Luke and Acts (see Colossians 4:14; 2 Timothy 4:11). This would make Luke the only Gentile to have written any books of the New Testament.

DATE: The Gospel of Luke was likely written between AD 59 and 63.

PURPOSE AND SUMMARY: Luke wrote to present Jesus as the Savior of the world, the compassionate healer and teacher. His careful historical approach is revealed in the preface, which states that the author has "carefully investigated everything from the beginning" (Luke 1:3). Unlike Mark, Luke includes an account of the virgin birth; and unlike Matthew, he extensively describes the Perean ministry of Jesus (see Luke 9–18).

The writer of this third Gospel was Doctor Luke, Paul's companion (see Acts 16:10-24; Colossians 4:14; 2 Timothy 4:11). He was a native of Syria and apparently was not a Jew, for Colossians 4:14 places him with other Gentile Christians. If this is true, he was the only Gentile writer of the New Testament books.

Luke's Gospel was written for the Greeks. Besides the Jews and the Romans, the Greeks were another people who had been preparing for Christ's coming. They differed from the other two groups, though, in that they possessed a wider culture and loved beauty, rhetoric and philosophy. Luke, an educated Greek himself and a keen observer, would be well suited for this task. Luke presents Jesus as the ideal of perfect manliness.

Notice that inspiration does not destroy individuality. In the introduction, Luke 1:1-4, the human element is seen in connection with God's revelation. Luke addressed his Gospel to a man named Theophilus. It is thought he was an influential Christian layman in Greece.

- Matthew presents Christ as King, to the Jews.
- Mark presents Christ as the servant of Jehovah, to the Romans.
- Luke presents Christ as the perfect man, to the Greeks.

Luke is the Gospel for the sinner. It brings out Christ's compassionate love in becoming Man to save humankind.

GENERAL CHARACTERISTICS OF LUKE'S GOSPEL

In Luke, we see God manifest in the flesh. Luke deals with the humanity of our Lord. He reveals the Savior as a man with all His sympathies, feelings and growing powers—a Savior suited to all. In this Gospel, we see the God of glory coming down to our level, experiencing how we live and subject to the same circumstances.

Luke's Gospel is the Gospel of Christ's manhood. This we must know, however: Although Jesus mingles with humanity, He is in sharp contrast to people. He was the solitary God-Man. There was as great a difference between Christ as the Son of man and we as the sons and daughters of men, as Christ as the Son of God and we as the sons and daughters of God. The difference is not merely relative but absolute. Let me make this fact clear: Read the words of the angel to Mary: "So the holy one to be born" (Luke 1:35); this refers to our Lord's humanity. It is in contrast to ours. Our human nature is unclean (see Isaiah 64:6), but the Son of God, when He became incarnate (took bodily form), was "holy." Adam in his unfallen state was innocent, but Christ was holy.

Distinctions

In keeping with the theme of his Gospel, Doctor Luke has given us the most complete details concerning the miraculous birth of Jesus. We are grateful that our chief testimony concerning this fact comes from a physician. Christ, the Creator of this universe, entered this world like any other person. It is a mystery of mysteries, but enough facts are given to let us see that the predictions came true.

Luke alone tells the story of the visit from the shepherds (see Luke 2:8-20).

We learn from this Gospel that as a boy, Jesus developed normally (see Luke 2:40,52). There is no mention of unhealthy or supernatural growth. As a child, He was to obey His earthly parents, Joseph and Mary (see Luke 2:51). Only Luke tells of Jesus' visit to the Temple when He was 12 years old.

As a man, Jesus toiled with His hands, wept over the city, kneeled in prayer and knew agony in suffering. All of these actions are strikingly human. Five out of six of the miracles were miracles of healing. Luke alone tells of Jesus healing Malchus's ear (see Luke 22:51).

Luke is the Gospel for the outcast on the earth. It is Luke who tells of the good Samaritan (see Luke 10:33), the publican (see Luke 18:13), the prodigal son (see Luke 15:11-24), Zacchaeus (see Luke 19:2) and the thief on the cross (see Luke 23:43). He is the writer who has the most to say for womanhood (see Luke 1–2). Luke records Jesus' compassion for the woman of Nain and the depths of His mercy for the woman who was a sinner. His regard for women and children is shown repeatedly (see Luke 7:46; 8:3; 8:42; 9:38; 10:38-42; 11:27; 23:27).

Luke alone tells us about the bloody sweat in Gethsemane; the walk with two disciples to Emmaus; Jesus' leading His disciples out as far as Bethany and that as He lifted up His hands and blessed them, He was parted from them.

Poetry

Luke is a poetic book. It opens with a song, "Glory to God" (Luke 2:14). It closes with a song, "Praising God" (Luke 24:53). The world has been singing ever since. Thank God for such a Gospel! It preserves the precious gems of Christian hymnology:

- The Magnificat—Mary's hymn of rejoicing—Luke 1:46-55
- Song of Zacharias—Luke 1:68-79
- Song of the angels—Luke 2:8-14

Prayers

Luke tells us more of the prayers of our Lord than any other Gospel writer. Prayer is the expression of human dependence on God. Why do so many in the Church appear to be working, yet so few people appear to be reached for God? Why does there appear to be so much activity, but so few are brought to Christ? The answer is simple: There is not enough private prayer. The cause of Christ does not need less working but more praying.

Universality

The hardest thing the Early Church had to learn was that the Gentiles would have full and free admission into the Kingdom and

Luke

into the Church. Simeon taught this. Read Luke 2:32. Christ sent the 70 disciples not to the lost sheep of the house of Israel alone, as Matthew says, who wrote especially for the Jews, but "to every town and place" (Luke 10:1). All of Jesus' ministry over the eastern side of Jordan was to the Gentiles.

OLD TESTAMENT PROMISE AND NEW TESTAMENT FULFILLMENT

I will extol the Lord at all times; his praise will always be on my lips. My soul will boast in the Lord; let the afflicted hear and rejoice.

PSALM 34:1-2

Though the Lord is on high, he looks upon the lowly, but the proud he knows from afar.

PSALM 138:6

Yet I will rejoice in the Lord, I will be joyful in God my Savior.

HABAKKUK 3:18

Mary said: "My soul glorifies the Lord and my spirit rejoices in God my Savior, for he has been mindful of the humble state of his servant. From now on all generations will call me blessed."

LUKE 1:46-48

LUKE 1–4:13: THE PREPARATION OF THE SON OF MAN

The opening of this beautiful book is significant. A man is to be described, and the writer, Luke, will teach his good friend Theophilus about Him. He tells Theophilus about his own personal knowledge of his subject: "since I myself have carefully investigated everything from the beginning" (Luke 1:3). He seems to bring something warmly human to his task of presenting the man Christ Jesus.

The opening chapter is characteristic of Luke's theme. John, as befits his theme, begins, "In the beginning was the Word, and the Word was with God, and the Word was God" (John 1:1). His tone throughout is not of this world, for he is presenting the story of the Son of God. But Luke, so different, begins his touching story about a man simply with, "In the time of Herod king of Judea there was a priest" (Luke 1:5). As the story progresses, we are introduced to human sympathies and relationships that none of the other Gospels tells us. We learn all about the circumstances that accompanied the birth and childhood of the holy babe and about the one who was sent as His forerunner. The birth of John the Baptist (see Luke 1:57-80), the angels' song to the shepherds (see Luke 2:8-20), the circumcision (see Luke 2:21), the presentation in the Temple (see Luke 2:22-38), and then the story of 12-year-old Jesus (see Luke 2:41-52) are all recorded here.

In chapter 2, Luke notes that "in those days Caesar Augustus issued a decree that a census should be taken of the entire Roman world" (Luke 2:1). Then comes a fact that we would never find in Matthew: Joseph and Mary "went to [Joseph's] own town to register" (Luke 2:3). Luke is not showing here One who has come to rule but One who has come in humility to be fully involved in human affairs.

God brings to pass what the prophets had spoken. Micah had said that Bethlehem was to be the birthplace of Jesus, for He was part of the family of David (see Micah 5:2-5). But Mary lived in Nazareth, a town 100 miles away. God saw to it that Imperial Rome issued a decree to compel Mary and Joseph to go to Bethlehem just as the child was to be born. Isn't it wonderful how God uses the decree of a pagan monarch to bring to pass His prophecy! God still moves the hand of rulers to do His bidding.

Now keep reading! Here's the message of the angels to the watching shepherds, but we do not find the kings of the East asking for One "who has been born king" (Matthew 2:2). The angel tells the poor shepherds, "I bring you good news that will cause great joy for all the people. Today in the town of David a Savior [not a King] has been born to you" (Luke 2:10-11).

Why did the Father allow His blessed Son to be born in this lowly place? Luke is the only one of the four evangelists who mentions this point about Jesus' humanity.

OLD TESTAMENT PROMISE AND NEW TESTAMENT FULFILLMENT

But showing love to a thousand generations of those who love me
and keep my commandments.

EXODUS 20:6

You save the humble, but your eyes are on the haughty to
bring them low.

2 SAMUEL 22:28

Sing to the Lord a new song, for he has done marvelous things; his right
hand and his holy arm have worked salvation for him.

PSALM 98:1

Our righteousness reaches to the skies, O God, you who have done
great things. Who, O God, is like you?

PSALM 107:9

He provided redemption for his people; he ordained his covenant forever—
holy and awesome is his name.

PSALM 111:9

For the Mighty One has done great things for me—holy is his name.
His mercy extends to those who fear him, from generation to generation.
He has performed mighty deeds with his arm; he has scattered
those who are proud in their inmost thoughts. He has brought down rulers
from their thrones but has lifted up the humble.

LUKE 1:49-52

Boyhood

"The child grew . . . and the grace of God was on him" (Luke 2:40). When Jesus was 12 years old, He went with His parents to Jerusalem to the Passover feast, as every Jewish boy did at that age. "The boy Jesus stayed behind in Jerusalem, but they were unaware of it" (Luke 2:43). How characteristic of a boy this is! He was found sitting among teachers, both listening to them and asking them questions (see Luke 2:46). How intensely human this is! Yet we read, "Everyone who heard him was amazed at his understanding and his answers" (Luke 2:47). Luke says that Jesus was filled with wisdom. Side by side with humans, He was always more than a man. We find Jesus' first words here: "Didn't you know I had to be in my Father's house?" (Luke 2:49). This is the first self-witness to His deity.

Then we read, "Then he went down to Nazareth with them and was obedient to them," His earthly parents (Luke 2:51). "And Jesus grew in wisdom and stature, and in favor with God and man" (Luke 2:52). All of these things are peculiar to Jesus as a man, and Luke alone records them. It is important that we notice that Jesus was a favorite ("in favor") in Nazareth. It is not a sign that we are in God's grace when we are out of favor with others.

Eighteen years of silence followed. We read of John the Baptist preaching "a baptism of repentance for the forgiveness of sins" (Luke 3:3). Then Jesus came to be baptized. Luke tells us, "When all the people were being baptized, Jesus was baptized too. And as he was praying, heaven was opened" (Luke 3:21). Jesus is linked with "all the people." He came down to the level of humans. Here only do we read of the age at which our Lord entered His public ministry (see Luke 3:23).

Genealogy

The genealogy of Jesus in Luke is given at the time of His baptism and not at His birth (see Luke 3:23). There are noticeable differences between the genealogy in Luke and the one found in Matthew 1. Each is significant!

- In Matthew we have the royal genealogy of the Son of David through Joseph—in Luke we have a strictly personal genealogy through Mary.

- Matthew establishes Jesus' legal line of descent through Joseph; while Luke establishes Jesus' lineal descent through Mary.

- In Matthew Jesus' genealogy is traced forward from Abraham; in Luke it is followed backward to Adam.

- Matthew shows us Jesus' relation to the Jewish people; hence, he goes back no further than to Abraham, father of the Jewish nation—Luke shows us Jesus' connection to the human race; hence, he goes back to Adam, the father of the human family.

In Luke our Lord's line is traced back to Adam and is, no doubt, His mother's line. Notice that Luke 3:23 does not say that Jesus was the son of Joseph. What are the words? "So it was thought." In Matthew 1:16, where Joseph's genealogy is given, we learn that Joseph was the son of Jacob. Luke says that Joseph was the son of Heli. Joseph could not be the natural son of two men. But note that Luke's record does not state that Heli sired Joseph, so it is supposed that Joseph was the son by law (or son-in-law) of Heli. Heli is believed to have been Mary's father.

In Luke, the Davidic genealogy goes through Nathan, not Solomon. This too is important. The Messiah must be David's son and heir, "a descendant of David" (Romans 1:3; see also 2 Samuel 7:12-13; Acts 2:30-31). He must literally be a flesh-and-blood descendant. Hence Mary must be a member of David's house as well as Joseph's (see Luke 1:32).

"Jesus, full of the Holy Spirit, left the Jordan and was led by the Spirit into the wilderness, where for forty days he was tempted by the devil" (Luke 4:1-2). Only in Luke do we learn that the Savior was "full of the Holy Spirit" as He returned from His baptism. Then the account of His temptation is given. Notice that Luke is the only one to tell us that "Jesus returned to Galilee in the power of the Spirit" (Luke 4:14), showing that the old serpent (Satan) had utterly failed to break the fellowship between the Son of man on earth and His Father in heaven.

Just as Jesus came forth from the fire of testing in the unquenchable "power of the Spirit," so too can we. Only as we are filled with His Spirit can we overcome temptation with the power of the Spirit.

OLD TESTAMENT PROMISE AND NEW TESTAMENT FULFILLMENT

I swear by myself, declares the Lord, that because you have done this and have not withheld your son, your only son, I will surely bless you and make your descendants as numerous as the stars in the sky and as the sand on the seashore. Your descendants will take possession of the cities of their enemies, and through your offspring all nations on earth will be blessed, because you have obeyed me.

GENESIS 22:16-18

He has remembered his love and his faithfulness to the house of Israel; all the ends of the earth have seen the salvation of our God.

PSALM 98:3

For he satisfies the thirsty and fills the hungry with good things.

PSALM 107:9

He has filled the hungry with good things but has sent the rich away empty. He has helped his servant Israel, remembering to be merciful to Abraham and his descendants forever, even as he said to our fathers.

LUKE 1:53-55

The purpose of the temptation was not to discover whether Jesus would give in to Satan but to demonstrate that He could not; the temptation illustrates the fact that there was nothing in Jesus to which Satan could appeal (see John 14:30). Christ could be tried and proven. The more you crush a rose, the more its fragrance is recognized. So the more the devil assaulted Christ, the more His perfections were revealed.

LUKE 4:14–19: THE MINISTRY OF THE SON OF MAN

Scan Luke 4:14–19, and find the events in Jesus' life as they are recorded in succession.

Jesus' Ministries

Jesus' ministry around Galilee is recorded in 4:14 to 9:50:

- Ministry in Nazareth, His hometown—Luke 4:16-30
- Preaching in Capernaum—Luke 4:31-44
- Call of Peter, James and John—Luke 5:1-11
- Call of Matthew—Luke 5:27-39
- Dealings with the Pharisees—Luke 6:1-11
- The choosing of the 12 apostles—Luke 6:12-16
- Teaching of the disciples—Luke 6:17-49
- Performance of miracles—Luke 7:1-17
- Discourses of the teacher—Luke 7:18-50
- Parables of the teacher—Luke 8:4-18
- Relatives of Jesus—Luke 8:19-21
- Calming of the sea—Luke 8:22-25
- Healing of the demon-possessed man—Luke 8:26-40
- Healing of the bleeding woman—Luke 8:43-48
- Restoration of Jairus's daughter—Luke 8:49-56
- Commissioning of the Twelve—Luke 9:1-10
- Feeding of the five thousand—Luke 9:10-17
- Confession by Peter—Luke 9:18-21

- Transfiguration of Jesus—Luke 9:27-36
- Healing of a lunatic—Luke 9:37-43

Jesus' ministry in Judea is recorded in 9:51–19:27:

- Commissioning of the 72—Luke 10:1-24
- Question of the lawyer—Luke 10:25-37
- Martha and Mary at home—Luke 10:38-42
- Teaching about praying—Luke 11:1-13
- Seeking signs from heaven—Luke 11:14-36
- Warnings about the Pharisees—Luke 12:1-12
- The sin of greed—Luke 12:13-59
- Teaching about repentance—Luke 13:1-9
- The kingdom of heaven—Luke 13:18-30
- Talks on hospitality—Luke 14:1-24
- Talks on self-denial—Luke 14:25-35
- Love of the lost—Luke 15
- Planning for the future—Luke 16:1-30
- Jesus' journey to Jerusalem—Luke 16:31–19:27

Jesus' Jerusalem ministry is found in Luke 19:28–24:

- Entry into Jerusalem—Luke 19:28-38
- Explanation of His authority—Luke 20–21:4
- Discussion of future things—Luke 21:5-38
- Eating of the last Passover—Luke 22:1-38
- Betrayal by Judas—Luke 22:39-53
- Trial before the high priest—Luke 22:54-71
- Trial before Pilate—Luke 23:1-26
- Crucifixion with two criminals—Luke 23:27-49
- Burial in the tomb—Luke 23:50-56
- Resurrection from the dead—Luke 24:1-48
- Ascension into heaven—Luke 24:49-53

This list is not complete, of course, but it gives a bird's-eye view of the busy life of the Son of man on earth. The keyword of His ministry is "compassion."

The Upbringing of a Man

Following the temptation, Jesus "went to Nazareth, where he had been brought up, and on the Sabbath day he went into the synagogue, as was his custom. And he stood up to read" (Luke 4:16). He went to the place where He had been "brought up." Upbringing is an important experience in life. We find that Jesus was accustomed to going to the synagogue on the Sabbath day, which implies that He had been reared in a godly home.

At the synagogue, Jesus stated that God had anointed Him to preach deliverance to the captives and to bring good tidings to the poor and brokenhearted (see Luke 4:18-19). He selected a text from Isaiah 61:1-2, which announced the object of His whole mission on earth. He was commissioned and sent by God, and He was divinely qualified for His work. He is our Kinsman-Redeemer. He was made like us so that He could save us. He became a man so that He could bring humankind close to God.

At this very early point in Jesus' ministry, we see that people in His hometown synagogue decided to kill Him (see Luke 4:28-30). They said, "Isn't this Joseph's son?" (Luke 4:22). This is the first hint of His future rejection. He proclaimed Himself to be the Messiah (see Luke 4:21). But they were angered because He hinted that their Messiah would also be sent to the Gentiles (see Luke 4:24-30). They believed God's grace was to be confined only to their own kind of people, so they were ready to kill Him. He refused to work miracles for them because of their unbelief. They attempted to throw Him off a cliff, but He escaped and went to Capernaum (see Luke 4:29-31). (By comparing Luke 4:16 with Matthew 13:54, it would seem that Jesus made another visit to Nazareth some months later, but He again met with opposition.)

A Gospel for the World

The Jewish people hated the Gentiles for their treatment of them when they were captives in Babylon. They regarded Gentiles with contempt and considered them unclean and enemies of God. Luke pictures Jesus as tearing down these barriers between Jew and Gentile, making repentance and faith the only conditions of admission to the Kingdom: "And repentance for the forgiveness of sins will be preached in his name to all nations, beginning at Jerusalem" (Luke 24:47). The gospel of Jesus Christ is not just one of the religions of the world. It is the living truth of God, adapted to all nations and to all classes. Read Romans 1:16.

As the Son of man, Christ looked at the needs of the Gentiles just as He looked at the needs of all people. In Luke 6, which in substance is the same as the Sermon on the Mount in Matthew, we find simple broad moral teachings, suited to the needs and wants of all people. Luke condenses into a few verses what Matthew puts into chapters 5 through 7 (see Luke 6:20-49). He makes only a passing reference to "the Law and the Prophets" (Luke 16:16), whereas Matthew emphasizes them (Matthew 7:12; 22:40).

Service of the Self

When the Twelve are commissioned, a broader field of ministry begins (see Luke 9). In Matthew we hear the Lord saying, "Do not go among the Gentiles or enter any town of the Samaritans. Go rather to the lost sheep of Israel" (Matthew 10:5-6). Luke omits this and says, "He sent them out to proclaim the kingdom of God and to heal the sick. So they set out . . . proclaiming the good news and healing people everywhere" (Luke 9:2,6).

Wherever this man Christ Jesus went, a multitude followed Him and "tried to touch him, because power was coming from him and healing them all" (Luke 6:19). He gave of Himself. Our service must be the same.

We find Jesus' power over disease and death (see Luke 7:1-17); we find Him the sinner's friend; we find that He had come "to seek and to save the lost" (Luke 19:10). He is called "a friend of tax collectors and sinners" (Luke 7:34).

The School of the Lord

The scholars of the Lord's school are His disciples, taught and trained by Jesus to carry on His message (see Luke 6:12-16).

Graduation from the school is not necessarily easy. Requirements must be fulfilled. *The entrance requirement is easy.* There is no barrier of age, sex, race or color. "And whoever does not carry their cross and follow me cannot be my disciple" (Luke 14:27). "Those of you who do not give up everything you have cannot be my disciples" (Luke 14:33). Read Luke 14:25-33.

OLD TESTAMENT PROMISE AND NEW TESTAMENT FULFILLMENT

The Spirit of the Sovereign Lord is on me, beause the Lord has anointed me to preach good news to the poor. He has sent me to bind up the brokenhearted, to proclaim freedom for the captives and release from darkness for the prisoners, to proclaim the year of the Lord's favor and the day of vengeance of our God, to comfort all who mourn

ISAIAH 61:1-2

"The Spirit of the Lord is on me, because he has anointed me to preach good news to the poor. He has sent me to proclaim freedom for the prisoners and recovery of sight for the blind, to release the oppressed, to proclaim the year of the Lord's favor." Then he rolled up the scroll, gave it back to the attendant and sat down. The eyes of everyone in the synagogue were fastened on him, and he began by saying to them, "Today this scripture is fulfilled in your hearing."

LUKE 4:18-21

The examinations are not the same for everyone. Jesus knows the ability and weakness of each student in His school, and He gives individual tests.

It is easy to follow Jesus' tests with Peter. In Luke 5, He tested Peter on obedience (see Luke 5:5). In Luke 9:18, Jesus gave a surprise quiz, and Peter gave a startling answer (see Luke 9:18-20).

There are a set of rules to be observed, and a right relationship with the teacher must be maintained at all times. Many people think that simply having established a relationship with the great teacher is all that is necessary, but this is not true. There must be a constant study of His Word, a laboratory time of prayer (see Luke 11:1-4), and time spent in the gym for spiritual exercises (see Luke 5:27; 9:59).

There is a practice school, where students show off the skills they have learned. Jesus not only taught His disciples, but He also made them try out the lessons He had taught them (see Luke 10:1-12, 28,36-37; 11:35; 12:8-9; 14:25-33; 18:18-26).

The course work is always the same. All classes focus on a study of the Kingdom and the King (see Luke 7:28; 8:1; 9:2,11,62; 12:32; 13:20-21,28-29; 17:20; 18:29; 19:12,15; 22:29).

LUKE 20–23: THE SUFFERING OF THE SON OF MAN

Jesus is sitting with His disciples around the table, celebrating the feast of the Passover. At this time, He institutes what we call the Lord's Supper. Listen to His words: "This is my body given for you . . . the new covenant in my blood, which is poured out for you" (Luke 22:19-20). This is different from the account in Matthew and Mark. They say, "My blood . . . which is poured out for many" (Matthew 26:28; Mark 14:24). His love is expressed in such a personal way in Luke. The evangelist adds: "Do this in remembrance of me" (Luke 22:19).

Read about the sad record of events in connection with Jesus' death. We find the disciples arguing over which one of them would be counted greatest in the Kingdom (see Luke 22:24-27). We follow Peter and we read a lamentable story—one that ends in Peter's denial of his Lord and Master (see Luke 22:54-62).

Look into the Garden of Gethsemane. Jesus is praying; and "as it were" (*KJV*), great drops of blood were on His holy brow (see Luke 22:44). Luke tells us that the angels came to minister to Him, the Son of man (see Luke 22:43). Matthew and Mark don't mention the ministering angels.

In the shadows of the garden, a contingent of soldiers approaches; leading them is Judas (see Luke 22:47). He steps up to kiss Jesus. Why, yes, he was a disciple. But the Scriptures had said that Jesus would be betrayed by a friend and sold for 30 pieces of silver (see Luke 22:47-62; Psalm 41:9; Zechariah 11:12).

Worst of all for Jesus, all but one of His friends desert Him. All flee, except John the beloved. Luke alone tells us that Jesus looks on Peter, the denier, and broke Peter's heart with His look of love (see Luke 23:61).

OLD TESTAMENT PROMISE AND NEW TESTAMENT FULFILLMENT

Even my close friend, whom I trusted, he who shared my bread,
has lifted up his heel against me.

PSALM 41:9

Then Satan entered Judas, called Iscariot, one of the Twelve.
And Judas went to the chief priests and the officers of the temple guard
and discussed with them how he might betray Jesus.

LUKE 22:3-4

We follow Jesus into Pilate's hall and then before Herod (see Luke 23:1-12). We follow along the Via Dolorosa ("way of suffering") to the cross (see Luke 23:27-38). Only Luke mentions the name "Calvary" (*KJV*), which is the Latin name for "Golgotha" ("place of a skull").

There were three crosses on the hill. On one of them was a thief, dying for his crimes. Luke tells us this story, too (see Luke 23:39-45). The way this thief was saved is the way every sinner must be saved. He believed in the Lamb of God who died on the cross that day to pay the penalty for our sins.

The scene closes with the Son of man crying with a loud voice, "Father, into your hands I commit my spirit" (Luke 23:46). The centurion, in keeping with this Gospel, vindicates Jesus: "Surely this was a righteous man" (Luke 23:47).

LUKE 24: THE VICTORY OF THE SON OF MAN

We turn with great relief from the sorrow and death associated with the cross, and the darkness and gloom of the tomb, to the brightness and glory of the resurrection morning. Luke gives us a part of the scene the other authors don't mention. It is the story of the walk to Emmaus.

Luke shows that Jesus, as the disciples' resurrected Lord, is just the same loving, understanding friend He had been before His death. After Jesus' walk and conversation with them, these disciples urged Him to come in and spend the night with them. He revealed who He was when He broke the bread. Then they recognized who He was, but He vanished out of their sight. After they returned to Jerusalem, they found abundant proof of His resurrection and of His being a real man with flesh and bones.

Eleven appearances of Jesus following His resurrection are recorded—not only to individuals, but also to small groups and crowds. First, to the women, to Mary and then to the others (see Mark 16; John 20:14): to Peter alone (see Luke 24:34); to two men walking to Emmaus (see Luke 24:13); to 10 apostles in Jerusalem (see John 20:19; Thomas was absent); to the 11 remaining disciples (see John 20:26,29); to seven men at the sea of Tiberias (see John 21:1); to all of the apostles on a mountain in Galilee (see Matthew 28:16); to 500 brethren at once (see 1 Corinthians 15:6); to James (see 1 Corinthians 15:7); and finally to the little group on the Mount of Olives at His ascension (see Luke 24:51).

Three times, we are told, His disciples touched Him when He appeared (see Matthew 28:9; Luke 24:39; John 20:27). He ate with them, too (see Luke 24:42; John 21:12-13). Finally, as Jesus raised His hands to bless them, "he . . . was taken up into heaven" (Luke 24:51).

Jesus is no longer a local Christ, confined to Jerusalem; He is a universal Christ. He could say to His disciples who mourned for Him and who thought that because He had died, He could no longer be with them, "And surely I am with you always" (Matthew 28:20). How different was the hope and joy of those chosen followers from their despair and shame at the Crucifixion! They returned to Jerusalem with great joy.

5

Understanding John

John Portrays Jesus Christ, the Son of God

AUTHOR: John 21:20 describes the author as "the disciple whom Jesus loved," and for both historical and internal reasons, this is understood to be John the apostle, one of the sons of Zebedee (see Luke 5:10).

DATE: Discovery of certain papyrus fragments dated around AD 135 require the Gospel of John to have been written, copied and circulated before then. And while some think the Gospel of John was written before Jerusalem was destroyed (AD 70), AD 85-90 is a more accepted date for its writing.

PURPOSE AND SUMMARY: The Gospel of John explains the mystery of the person of Christ by the use of the term *Logos* ("Word") and was written to convince readers that Jesus was the Christ, the Son of God (see John 20:31). John not only records events in Jesus' life and ministry, as do the other Gospels, but John also uniquely interprets the events by showing their deeper, spiritual meaning. The author makes significant use of such images as light, water, life, love and bread to describe the life and presence of God that Jesus brings to every believer.

The purpose of this book is stated by the author in the book's opening 18 verses, the prologue, and he states it very plainly in John 20:31. John wrote to prove that Jesus was the Christ, the promised Messiah (for the Jews) and the Son of God (for the Gentiles), and to lead believers into a life of divine friendship with Him. "Messiah" means "anointed One, who comes as divine King." The keyword is "believe." We find this word in one form or another more than 90 times in this book.

The theme of John's Gospel is the deity of Jesus Christ. More here than anywhere else Jesus' divine Sonship is set forth. In this Gospel, we are shown that the baby of Bethlehem was none other than "the one and only Son, who came from the Father" (John 1:14). John reveals the great deal of evidence that proves this truth. Although "all things were made" by Him (John 1:3) and although "in him was life" (John 1:4), He "became flesh and made his dwelling among us" (John 1:14). No person can see God; therefore, Christ came to declare Him—to be living proof of His existence. John leaves out of his story many things that are found in the other Gospels:

- No genealogy—neither Jesus' legal lineage through Joseph (as given by Matthew), nor His personal descent through Mary (as given by Luke)
- No account of Jesus' birth—because He was "in the beginning" (John 1:1)
- Nothing about Jesus' boyhood
- Nothing about Jesus' temptation
- No Transfiguration

- No appointing of Jesus' disciples
- No parables
- No account of the Ascension
- No Great Commission

Yet only in John is Jesus called:

- "The Word" (John 1:1)
- The Creator (see John 1:3)
- "The only begotten of the Father" (John 1:14, *KJV*)
- "The Lamb of God" (John 1:29,36)
- "I am" (John 8:58)—the revelation of the great "I AM" (Exodus 3:14)

The author of this Gospel was John, "son of thunder," "the disciple whom Jesus loved" (John 13:23; 21:7,20). His father was Zebedee, a successful fisherman; his mother was Salome, a devout follower of the Lord who may have been a sister of Mary, the mother of Jesus (see Mark 15:40; John 19:25). His brother was James. His position was probably somewhat better than that of an ordinary fisherman.

John may have been about 25 years of age when Jesus called him. He had been a follower of John the Baptist. During the reign of the Roman Emperor Domitian, John the disciple was banished to Patmos, but afterward he returned to Ephesus and became the pastor of the wonderful church there. He lived to an extreme old age in that city, the last of the 12 apostles. During this time, he wrote his Gospel concerning the deity of the Christ, co-eternal with the Father.

John wrote nearly a generation after the other evangelists, somewhere between AD 80 and 100, at the end of the first century when all of the New Testament was complete except for his own writings. The life and work of Jesus were well known at this time. The gospel had been preached, Paul and Peter had suffered martyrdom, and all the other apostles had died. Jerusalem had been destroyed by the Roman legions under Titus, AD 70.

John

OLD TESTAMENT PROMISE AND NEW TESTAMENT FULFILLMENT

No man can see Me and live!

EXODUS 33:20, *NASB*

The Word became flesh and made his dwelling among us. We have seen his glory, the glory of the One and Only, who came from the Father, full of grace and truth.

JOHN 1:14

All the Synoptic Gospels (Matthew, Mark and Luke) were written before AD 70, the fateful year of the overthrow of Jerusalem. By then, false teachers had begun to deny that Jesus Christ was the Son of God who had come in the form of a man. John, therefore, wrote to prove those facts, recording eyewitness accounts and the words and works of Jesus that reveal His divine power and glory.

GENERAL CHARACTERISTICS OF JOHN'S GOSPEL

John's Gospel is more elevated in tone and more exalted in view than the other Gospels. In each of the first three Gospels, Christ is viewed in human relationship with an earthly people, but in John we find spiritual relationships with a heavenly people.

In Matthew and Luke, "Son of David" and "Son of man" link Christ to the earth. In John, "Son of God" connects Him with the Father in heaven.

Luke takes care to guard our Lord's divine perfection in His humanity; John takes care to guard Jesus' divine perfection in His deity. In these days of widespread departure from the truth, the deity of Christ Jesus must be emphasized.

In John, Jesus is shown dwelling with God before any creature was formed (see John 1:1-2). He is distinguished as "the glory of the one and only" (John 1:14). "This is God's Chosen One" (John 1:34).

More than 20 times, Jesus speaks of God as "my Father." Twenty-five times He says, "Verily, verily" (*KJV*)—speaking with authority. Besides His own affirmation, six different witnesses attest to His deity.

JESUS' DEITY

In every chapter of the book of John, we see Jesus' deity:

- John 1—In his confession, Nathanael said, "You are the Son of God" (verse 49).
- John 2—In the miracle of Cana, "he revealed his glory" (verse 11).
- John 3—In His word to Nicodemus, He said that He was "his one and only Son" (the "only begotten Son," *KJV*) (verse 16).
- John 4—In His conversation with the woman of Samaria, He stated, "I, the one speaking to you—I am [the Messiah]" (verse 26).
- John 5—To the impotent man, He disclosed that "the voice of the Son of God" will call the dead to life (verse 25).
- John 6—He admitted, "I am the bread of life" (verse 35).
- John 7—He proclaimed, "Let anyone who is thirsty come to me and drink" (verse 37).
- John 8—To the unbelieving Jews, He disclosed, "Before Abraham was born, I am!" (verse 58).
- John 9—The blind man was told, "You have now seen [the Son of man]; in fact, he is the one speaking with you"— Jesus' unique claim to being the Son of God (verse 37).
- John 10—Jesus stated, "I and the Father are one" (verse 30).
- John 11—Martha declared, "You are the Messiah, the Son of God" (verse 27).

John

- John 12—To the Greeks, He said, "I, when I am lifted up from the earth, will draw all people to myself" (verse 32).
- John 13—At the Last Supper, He said, "You call me 'Teacher' and 'Lord,' and rightly so, for that is what I am" (verse 13).
- John 14—He stated, "You believe in God; believe also in me" (verse 1).
- John 15—Likening us to branches on a vine, He said, "Apart from me you can do nothing" (verse 5).
- John 16—In promising the Holy Spirit, He said, "I will send him to you" (verse 7).
- John 17—He said, "Glorify your Son" (verse 1).
- John 18—During His trial, He stated, "You say that I am a king" (verse 37).
- John 19—In His atonement, He had the right to say, "It is finished" (verse 30).
- John 20—In his confession, Thomas the doubter exclaimed, "My Lord and my God!" (verse 28).
- John 21—In demanding obedience, He said, "You must follow me" (verse 22).

John

Seven Witnesses

John brings seven witnesses to the stand to prove that Jesus Christ was God. Turn to the Scriptures, and imagine each one making his or her own statement:

1. What do you say, John the Baptist? "This is God's Chosen One" (John 1:34).
2. What is your conclusion, Nathanael? "You are the Son of God" (John 1:49).
3. What do you know, Peter? "You are the Holy One of God" (John 6:69).
4. What do you think, Martha? "You are the Messiah, the Son of God" (John 11:27).
5. What is your verdict, Thomas? "My Lord and my God!" (John 20:28).

6. What is your statement, John? "Jesus is the Messiah, the Son of God" (John 20:31).
7. What do You say of Yourself, Christ? "I am God's Son" (John 10:36).

OLD TESTAMENT PROMISE AND NEW TESTAMENT FULFILLMENT

You will be like a well-watered garden, like a spring whose waters never fail.

ISAIAH 58:11

If anyone is thirsty, let him come to me and drink. Whoever believes in me, as the Scripture has said, streams of living water will flow from within him

JOHN 7:37-38

Seven Miracles

Besides the seven witnesses John calls on, he describes seven signs, or miracles, that prove Jesus was God. "For no one could perform the signs you are doing if God were not with him," were Nicodemus's words (John 3:2).

Look over these signs as they occur throughout the book:

1. Turning water into wine—John 2:1-11
2. Healing the nobleman's son—John 4:46-54
3. Healing the man at Bethesda—John 5:1-47
4. Feeding the five thousand—John 6:1-14
5. Walking on water—John 6:15-21
6. Healing the blind man—John 9:1-41
7. Raising Lazarus—John 11:1-57

Seven "I AM"s

There is yet another proof of Jesus' deity. Jesus reveals His God-nature in the "I am"s of this book:

1. "I am the bread of life"—John 6:35.
2. "I am the light of the world"—John 8:12.
3. "Before Abraham was born, I am"—John 8:58.
4. "I am the good shepherd"—John 10:11.
5. "I am the resurrection and the life"—John 11:25.
6. "I am the way and the truth and the life"—John 14:6.
7. "I am the true vine"—John 15:1.

John, only, records the triumphant shout, "It is finished" (John 19:30). The finished work of salvation is accomplished only by the Son of God.

JOHN 1:1-18: THE GREAT PROLOGUE

We open the book of John with this question in mind: "What do you think of Christ?" (see Matthew 22:42). Was He only the world's greatest teacher, or is He actually God? Was He one of the prophets, or is He the world's Savior whose coming was foretold by the prophets?

All of this prologue deals with Christ before His incarnation. God did not send Christ into the world so that He would become His Son. Christ *is* the eternal Son. He is the eternal Word. Jesus is none other than the Jehovah of the Old Testament, God manifest in the flesh. In Luke we see Christ going down to meet people's needs; in John we see Him drawing people up to Himself (see John 12:32).

All that John plans to discuss in his book is crowded into the first 18 verses. Let us study this Gospel with John's purpose clearly in mind, so read John 20:31 again. Let us see how the plan is developed and how the purpose is shown as we read the book.

The Son of God

Comparing the first verses of John with the beginning of the other three Gospels, we see how differently it opens, how exalted is its theme. Read John 1:1-18 carefully.

John does not open with the birth of Jesus (which connotes the Son of man) but before all worlds were formed. John begins, "In the beginning was the Word" (John 1:1). It opens like the book of Genesis opens! Jesus is portrayed as the Son of God before He became flesh and dwelled among us.

Our Lord had no beginning. He was in the beginning. He is eternal. Christ was before all things; therefore, Jesus is no part of creation—He *is* the Creator (see Colossians 1:16; Hebrews 1:2).

"The Word was with God" (John 1:1). Jesus is the Second Person of the Triune God (God the Father, God the Son, God the Holy Spirit). He is called "The Word." He came to declare God, to tell about God. As words give voice to thoughts, so Christ gives substance to God. Words reveal the heart and mind, so Christ expresses, manifests and shows God. Jesus said to Philip, "If you really know me, you will know my Father as well" (John 14:7).

Then comes the wonderful announcement that "through him all things were made; without him nothing was made that has been made. In him was life, and that life was the light of all mankind" (John 1:3-4). Yes, "The Word became flesh and made his dwelling among us" (John 1:14). The full claims of Christ are given here: truly God, light of life, declarer of God the Father, baptizer with the Holy Spirit.

Remember that John is writing to prove that Jesus is the Son of God.

The Son of Man

John's prologue points out the incarnation of Christ. Christ became what He was not previously—a man. But Christ did not cease to be God. He was God-Man. He lived in a tabernacle of flesh here in this world for 33 years. "Incarnation" comes from two Latin words, *in caro*, meaning "flesh." So Christ was God in the flesh.

People had sinned and no longer reflected the image of God, so Christ—"the image of the invisible God" (Colossians 1:15)—came to dwell with people. No person could see God; therefore, the only begotten Son who was "in the bosom of the Father" (John 1:18, *KJV*) came to literally embody Him for us.

Even the witness of John the Baptist is different in John's Gospel. According to Matthew, John the Baptist told of the coming Kingdom. According to Luke, he preached repentance. According to John, he was a witness to the light so that all people might believe (see John 1:7). John the Baptist pointed to "the Lamb of God" (John 1:36).

Jesus is God Himself in human form on earth. Jesus is the witness of the Father to humans. Jesus knows the Father. He lived with Him from the beginning. He came down to tell us what He knows. He wanted humans to know the Father as well as He knows Him.

And the way Jesus told us about God was through His words, His deeds, His character, His love and, most important of all, His dying on the cross and His rising on the third day. All this was an embodying, a witnessing, a telling.

How was Christ the Word received? Read John 1:11: "He came to that which was his own, but his own did not receive him." He presented Himself as Messiah and King to His people, but He was rejected. All through John's book, we see Jesus dividing the crowds. As He comes out and speaks the truth, the crowds listen. Some believe Him, and John presents the results of faith. Some in the crowd, however, reject what He has to say—tragedy indeed!

The Way of Salvation

John reveals to us the following about salvation:

- What must we do to receive salvation? You must believe and receive.
- What will be the result? You will become a child of God (see John 1:12).
- What are you not to count on for salvation? Yourself.

John

Sometimes the way to better understand what something is, is to find out what it is not. In John 1:13, John tells us what salvation is not: being born "of natural descent . . . of human decision or a husband's will." All of these things are what too many people are counting on today for eternal life. It is our "new birth" that makes us "children of God" (John 1:12). In verse 13, John makes four points about God's children:

1. "Not of natural descent"—heredity; how much we depend on good birth! But not where salvation is concerned!
2. "Nor of human decision"—culture and education; it is not what we know but whom we believe that saves us.
3. "Nor of the will of man" (*KJV*)—prestige or influence; it is not by human determination that we are saved.
4. "But born of God"—by the power of the Holy Spirit of God; God comes down and redeems us, if we will only believe and receive Him as Savior and Lord.

JOHN 1:19–12: PUBLIC MINISTRY

When John the Baptist appears on the scene, the great drama of John's Gospel begins. "Among those born of women there has not risen anyone greater than John the Baptist," Jesus declared (Matthew 11:11; see also Luke 7:28). John was the forerunner of the Messiah. In this Gospel, John the Baptist is not described. He merely testifies that Jesus is the Messiah (see John 1:18-34).

A delegation of priests and Levites were sent to ask John who he claimed to be. He told them that he was not the Messiah, and he was not Elijah or any other prophet Moses spoke of; he was merely "the voice of one calling in the wilderness, 'Make straight the way for the Lord' " (John 1:23).

The next day, when he sees Jesus, John points to Him and says, "Look, the Lamb of God" (John 1:29).

Then John the Baptist indicates that he knew Jesus was the Messiah because he saw "the Spirit come down from heaven as a dove and remain on him" (John 1:32). So John adds, "I have seen and I testify that this is God's Chosen One" (John 1:34).

OLD TESTAMENT PROMISE AND NEW TESTAMENT FULFILLMENT

God himself will provide the lamb for the burnt offering

GENESIS 22:8

Behold, the Lamb of God who takes away the sin of the world!

JOHN 1:29, *NASB*

Jesus' Signs

Jesus' disciples were convinced of His deity by His first miracle: turning water into wine. He spoke, and it was so. This was one of the big factors that caused the disciples to have faith and believe in Jesus. This miraculous act was the first sign to prove that He was the Messiah (see John 2:11).

The next sign that Jesus gave occurred when He cleared the Temple. There was only one place where Jesus could start His ministry—in Jerusalem, the capital city. Just before the Passover, the Lord entered the Temple, and using a whip as a badge of His authority, He cleared the sanctuary, which He declared was His "Father's house" (John 2:16). By this act, He claimed to be the true Son of God.

After Jesus cleared the Temple and drove out the money-changers, the rulers asked Jesus for a sign to prove His authority. Jesus answered, "Destroy this temple, and I will raise it again in three days" (John 2:19). The rulers were shocked, for it had taken 46 years to build the Temple. "But the temple he had spoken of was his body," John explains (John 2:21). The supreme proof of Christ's deity is the resurrection.

Jesus gave to Nicodemus the wonderful teachings about eternal life and His love (see John 3:16) and the new birth (see John 3:6). Nicodemus was a moral, upright man, yet Christ said to him, "You must be born again" (John 3:7). If Jesus had said this to the Samaritan woman, Nicodemus would have agreed with Him. She was not a Jew and could not expect anything on the grounds that she had been born a Samaritan. But Nicodemus was a Jew by birth, and he had a right to expect something on this basis alone. But it was to him Jesus said, "You must be born again" in order to enter the kingdom of heaven. (Have you been born again?)

OLD TESTAMENT PROMISE AND NEW TESTAMENT FULFILLMENT

Love the Lord your God with all your heart and with all your soul and with all your strength.

DEUTERONOMY 6:5

The Father judges no one, but has entrusted all judgment to the Son, that all may honor the Son just as they honor the Father. He who does not honor the Son does not honor the Father, who sent him.

JOHN 5:22-23

Like the Jewish people of his day, Nicodemus knew God's law but nothing of God's love. He recognized Jesus as a teacher, but he did not know Him as the Savior. This is what too many people in the world do today. They put Jesus at the head of the list of the teachers of the world but do not worship Him as the one true God. *Jesus revealed to one woman the truth of His Messiahship.* Jesus brought an immoral woman face to face with Himself and showed her what kind of life she was leading. Christ did not condemn her or pass judgment upon her, but He did reveal to her that He is the only One who could meet her needs. Christ revealed the wonderful truth to her that He is the water of life. He alone can satisfy. The wells of the world cannot provide satisfaction.

This woman's loose view of marriage is not unlike the view of marriage held by many people today. People try every kind of well—money, power, clothes, food, possessions, drugs—but they still are unhappy and unsatisfied.

Did the woman believe Christ? What did she do? Her actions spoke louder than any words could have. She went back to town, and by her simple testimony brought a whole town to Christ (see John 4:1-42). This story gives us Christ's estimate of a single soul.

Old Testament Promise and New Testament Fulfillment

When the dew settled on the camp at night, the manna also came down.

NUMBERS 11:9

I am the bread of life. He who comes to me will never go hungry, and he who believes in me will never be thirsty.

JOHN 6:35

By healing the son of a nobleman, Jesus gives another sign of His deity. During His interview with the centurion, Jesus brought him to an open confession of Christ as Lord—yes, and his whole household joined with him (see John 4:46-54).

The miracle of feeding five thousand was a parable in action rather than in words. Jesus Himself is the bread from heaven. He wanted to tell them that to all who put their trust in Him, He will give satisfaction and joy (see John 6:35).

The people wanted to make Christ their King because He could feed them. How like people today! They long for someone who can give them food and clothing. But Christ would not be King on their terms. He dismissed the excited multitude and went to a mountain. The people were disappointed that He would not be a political leader, so they "turned back and no longer followed him" (John 6:66).

The people were divided because of Jesus (see John 7:40-44). Unbelief was developing into actual hostility, but in His true followers, faith was growing. Some people said, "He is a good man." Others said, "Not so." We must say one or the other today as well. Either He is God or an impostor. There is no middle ground.

The healing of the blind man led Jesus to reveal to this fellow who He was. When "they threw him out" because of his confession of Christ (John 9:34), Jesus gave a great discourse on the Good Shepherd (see John 10). Read John 10:19-21 to learn the results produced by His words. Notice the accusations of blasphemy they made against Christ when He said, "I and the Father are one" (John 10:30). "Again his Jewish opponents picked up stones to stone him" (John 10:31). What happened in the face of all this criticism and opposition? Read John 10:42.

OLD TESTAMENT PROMISE AND NEW TESTAMENT FULFILLMENT

The Lord is my shepherd, I shall not be in want.

PSALM 23:1

I am the good shepherd; I know my sheep
and my sheep know me.

JOHN 10:14

The raising of Lazarus is the final sign in John's Gospel. The other Gospel authors tell about the raising of Jairus's daughter and the son of the widow of Nain. But John tells about Lazarus, a man who had been dead four days. In reality, would it be any harder for God to raise one than the other? Nevertheless, it had a profound effect on the leaders (see John 11:47-48). The great claim Jesus made for Himself to Martha is recorded here: "I am the resurrection and the life. He who believes in me will live, even though they die; and whoever lives by believing in me will never die. Do you believe this?" (John 11:25-26).

This scene closes with Jesus' triumphant entry into Jerusalem. His public ministry had come to an end. It is recorded that many of the chief Jewish leaders believed in Him but did not make a public confession of faith.

OLD TESTAMENT PROMISE AND NEW TESTAMENT FULFILLMENT

I know that my Redeemer lives, and that in the end he will stand upon the earth. And after my skin has been destroyed, yet in my flesh I will see God.

JOB 19:25-26

I am the resurrection and the life. He who believes in me will live, even though he dies

JOHN 11:25

Jesus' Startling Claims
Jesus claims to be equal with God. Jesus calls God "my Father" (John 5:17). The Jews knew what He meant. He made Himself equal with God, they said. They knew that He claimed God as His Father in a way that meant that He is not the Father of any other person.

Jesus claims to be the light of the world. Jesus said, "I am the light of the world. Whoever follows me will never walk in darkness, but will have the light of life" (John 8:12).

Jesus claims to be eternal with God. Jesus said, "Very truly I tell you . . . before Abraham was born, I am!" (John 8:58). This claim of eternity with God was unmistakable. He was either the Son of God or a deceiver. Indeed, He uses the "I AM" of God's personal name, equating Himself with the Father (Exodus 3:14). No wonder the Jews "picked up stones to stone him" (John 8:59).

JOHN 13–17: PRIVATE MINISTRY

With the beginning of John 13, we leave the multitude behind and follow Jesus as He lived the last week of His life on earth before His crucifixion. We call it Passion Week:

> Sunday—the triumphant entry into Jerusalem
> Monday—the cleansing of the Temple
> Tuesday—the conflicts in the Temple
> Evening—the discourse on the Mount of Olives
> Thursday—preparation for the Passover
> Evening—the Last Supper with His disciples

Last words are always important. Jesus is leaving His disciples and is giving them His last instructions. These chapters, John 13–17, are called the holy of holies of the Scriptures. Prayerfully read them all at one sitting.

Christ's Last Meal with the Disciples

Jesus divided the Jewish people—some believed Him, others rejected Him completely. Now before He left them, He gathered His own around Him in the Upper Room and told them many secrets. He wanted to comfort His disciples, for He knew how hard it would be for them when He was gone. They would be sheep without a shepherd.

It is wonderful that Jesus selected and loved men like these. With the exception of Peter and John, they were all "nobodies." But they were "His own," and He loved them (John 13:1). One of Jesus' specialties is to make "somebodies" out of "nobodies." This is what He did with His first group of followers, and this is what He has continued to do through the centuries.

OLD TESTAMENT PROMISE AND NEW TESTAMENT FULFILLMENT

God said to Moses, "I AM WHO I AM."

EXODUS 3:14

"I tell you the truth," Jesus answered, "before Abraham was born, I am!"

JOHN 8:58

What a picture we have in John 13:1-11! Jesus, the Son of God, has a towel around His waist, has a basin of water in His blessed hands and is washing His disciples' feet! He wants us to serve others in the same spirit. He taught us that greatness is always measured by service. There is no loving others without living for others (see verses 16-17). Christ said, "The greatest among you will be your servant" (Matthew 23:11).

Jesus foretells His betrayal by Judas (see John 13:18-30), and Judas goes out into the night. It was night in Judas's heart, too. Fellowship brings light. Sin brings darkness. What a pitiable picture Judas is! He had such a wonderful opportunity to get to know Jesus, but he rejected the Lord. This is what unbelief can do. Belief means light and life, while unbelief means darkness and death.

After announcing that He will be leaving, the Lord gives His disciples a new commandment: "A new command I give you: Love one another. As I have loved you, so you must love one another. By this everyone will know that you are my disciples, if you love one another" (John 13:34-35). Discipleship is tested not by the creed you recite, not by the hymns you sing, not by the rituals you observe, but by the fact that you love one another. The degree to which Christians love one another is the degree to which the world believes them and believes in their Christ. It is the final test of discipleship. Jesus mentions this new commandment again in John 15:12.

Christ's Promise of a Comforter

"I am going there to prepare. . . . I will come back and take you to be with me" (John 14:2-3). This is Jesus' cure for heart troubles—faith in God. How many hearts have been put to rest and how many eyes have been dried by these words in John 14!

Jesus had spoken of His Father, but now He speaks of the other person of the Godhead, the Holy Spirit. If He (Christ) is to go away, He will send the Comforter, and He will stay with them. This is a wonderful promise for the child of God! Jesus repeats the promise in chapter 15 and again in 16. Look up John 15:26; 16:13-15. Few know of this presence in their lives, but it is by His power that we live. Never call the Holy Spirit "it." He is a person. He is one of three persons in the Triune God (the Trinity).

Let us look at the teaching about the Holy Spirit as given to us by John:

1. The incoming Spirit (John 3:5)—This is the beginning of the Christian life, the new birth by the Spirit. We are born by the Spirit into the family of God.

2. The indwelling Spirit (John 4:14)—The Holy Spirit fills us with His presence and brings us joy.

3. The overflowing Spirit (John 7:38-39)—"Rivers of living water will flow from within him." Not just little

John

streams of blessing will flow but rivers—Mississippis and Amazons—if the Holy Spirit dwells within us.

4. The witnessing Spirit (John 14-16)—The Holy Spirit speaks through us. Testifying about Christ is a necessity that every Christian fulfills through the Holy Spirit.

"Peace I leave with you; my peace I give you" (John 14:27). This is Christ's legacy to us. The only peace we can enjoy in this world is His peace.

The Secret of Remaining

Jesus reveals the real secret of the Christian life to His disciples in John 15: "Remain in [Christ]" (John 15:4-10; "abide," *KJV*). He is the source of life. Remain in Christ as the branch remains in the vine. In order to bear fruit, the branch cannot sever itself from the vine and then reconnect itself at will to the trunk. It must remain in the vine if it wants to bear fruit. This is the picture of our lives in Christ. Live and walk in Christ and you will bear fruit. If you do not remain in Christ, the fruit will soon disappear.

After He ended His talk with the 11 disciples, Jesus spoke to the Father. The disciples listened to His loving and solemn words. How thrilled they must have been as He told the Father how much He loved them and how He cared for them! He mentioned everything about Himself that He had taught them. He would keep them (see John 17:11); He would sanctify them (see John 17:17); He would make them one (see John 17:21); and finally, He would let all His children share in His glory someday (see John 17:24).

If you truly want to experience the beauty and depth of these wonderful words, kneel and let the Son of God lead you in prayer as you read aloud this seventeenth chapter of John.

JOHN 18–19: SUFFERING AND DEATH

Immediately following His prayer, Jesus went to the Garden of Gethsemane, knowing full well what would happen to Him. The change from the scene in the Upper Room to the scene in the olive grove is like going from warmth to cold, from light to darkness. Only two hours had passed since Judas left the supper table. Now we see him betraying his best friend. Remember, Judas was not forced to betray his Lord—he personally chose to betray Christ, and this treacherous act fulfilled prophecy. God did not cause Judas to sin, but Judas's betrayal was prophesied because it was going to happen. No one has ever *had* to sin to carry out any of God's plan.

The final hours had come! The mission of our Lord on earth was ending. Only the greatest work of Christ remained to be done—His supreme, crowning act of His life on earth. It was not a crisis but a climax. He was to die so that He would glorify the Father and save the sinful world. He came to earth to "give his life as a ransom for many" (Matthew 20:28; Mark 10:45). Christ came into the world by the manger and left it by the door of the cross.

Jesus was now ready to give the Jews the real sign of His authority in answer to the question they had asked in chapter 2: " 'What sign can you show us to prove your authority to do all this?' Jesus answered them, 'Destroy this temple, and I will raise it again in three days' " (John 2:18-19).

We see Jesus, still poised, still gentle. He knew His hour had come. He was not surprised when He heard the soldiers approach. He stepped forward to meet them. The men retreated and fell before the majesty of His look.

A Willing Captive

Follow Him, bound as a captive, to the hall of the high priest. Jesus was the One in command of the situation all through this terrible drama. He went of His own accord, a voluntary sacrifice (see John 18:4). He deliberately tasted death for every person.

Almost as pathetic as Judas was Peter, the deserter in the hour of need, denying three times that he had any connection with his best friend! This is a lesson for us in overconfidence. Poor Peter is to be pitied, for he really loved the Master.

Peter did not know that the supreme trial of his life would come in the form of a question from a servant girl. This is often the case. We lock and bolt the main door, but the thief breaks in through a tiny window that we had not even thought of. We would die at the stake but deny Christ in our speech.

All the disciples but John deserted Jesus in the hour of His greatest need. (Peter denied Jesus, but he stayed close by.) Among those fleeing is James of the inner circle, Nathanael the guileless, and Andrew the personal worker. Yet, here they were, running as fast as they could down the road together, away from their friend. A sorry sight! But wait! Don't start blaming them. Look to see where you are. Are you following Jesus closely? Remember, the majority is not always right. Be sure you are right! Can Christ count on you?

The brief interval between Peter's denial and Jesus' climbing the hill to Golgotha was crowded with incidents. The night trial before Caiaphas and the Sanhedrin (a court of 70 religious rulers) probably preceded the last denial of Peter. Then came the awful scourging by the Romans, which was often so severe that prisoners died under the torturing blows. The crown of thorns that was thrust upon Jesus' holy brow was only another act of cruel torture. When He comes again, He will wear "many crowns" (Revelation 19:12).

Finally, Pilate led Him forth and said, "Here is the man!" (John 19:5). What a sight! To see the Creator of this universe, the light and life of the world, the holy One treated so! But Satan energized the religious rulers, and they cried, "Crucify! Crucify! . . . He claimed to be the Son of God" (John 19:6-7).

John

The Blackest Hour

Finally the make-believe trials are over. It is morning, yet it seems like night. It is the world's blackest hour. The courtyard is deserted. The fire at which Peter warmed himself is only gray ashes. The soldiers' jeers, Herod's sneers and Pilate's vacillation are over. At the cross, we have hate at its worst and love at its best. People so hated Christ that they put Him to death. God so loved the world that He gave people life.

Our religion is one of four letters instead of two. Other religions say "Do." Our religion says "Done." Our Savior has done all on the cross. He took on our sins; and when He gave up His life, He said, "It is finished" (John 19:30). This was the shout of a conqueror. He had finished humanity's redemption. Nothing was left for people to do. Has the work been done in your heart?

Jesus was crucified on Golgotha, "the place of the Skull" (John 19:17). He is crucified there today—in people's minds. They crucify Him afresh and put Him to an open shame. "Christ died for our sins" (1 Corinthians 15:3). Salvation is costly—it cost Jesus His life.

OLD TESTAMENT PROMISE AND NEW TESTAMENT FULFILLMENT

"This is the covenant I will make with the house of Israel after that time," declares the Lord. "I will put my law in their minds and write it on their hearts. I will be their God, and they will be my people."

JEREMIAH 31:33

And with that he breathed on them and said, "Receive the Holy Spirit."

JOHN 20:22

John

JOHN 20–21: VICTORY OVER DEATH

We have a Savior who is victorious over death. He "always lives" (Hebrews 7:25).

On the third day, the tomb was empty! The grave clothes were all in order. Jesus had risen from the dead but not as others had done. When Lazarus rose from the dead, he was still wrapped in his grave clothes. Jesus, however, came out in his natural body—he was not "a ghost" (Luke 24:39)—but His natural body had been changed into a spiritual body. The changed body came right out of its linen wrappings and left them behind in the same way that a butterfly leaves behind its chrysalis, or shell. Read what John says in 20:6-8.

Jesus' appearances, 11 in all after His resurrection, helped His disciples to believe that He was God. Read John 20:28, the confession of the sixth witness, Thomas the doubter. Jesus wanted every doubt to be removed from each one of His disciples, because they must carry out His Great Commission to carry the gospel to all the world (see John 20:21).

Jesus gave the disciple who three times had denied Him, Peter, three opportunities to confess Him (see John 21:15-19). He restored Peter to full privileges of service again. Christ only wants those who love Him to serve Him. And if you love Him, you must serve Him. No one who loves Christ can help but serve.

What are Jesus' last words in this Gospel? "You must follow me" (John 21:22). This is His word to each one of us. May we all follow Him in loving obedience "until he comes" (1 Corinthians 11:26; see also Matthew 26:29).

A. J. Gordon, founder of Gordon College, once aptly summed up the Gospel of John in one sentence: "This Gospel opens with Christ in the bosom of the Father, and closes with John in the bosom of Christ."

WAYS TO REMEMBER THE BOOK OF JOHN

There are various ways of remembering the contents of the book of John. We will list only two here.

Use the Human Element
One way to remember the contents of John's Gospel is to memorize humanity's opinion of the Son of God:

- What individuals thought about Christ—John 1–5
- What Christ said about Himself—John 6–10
- What crowds thought of Christ—John 11–20

Use the Three Keys

Dr. S. D. Gordon, an American author, once suggested that three keys be used to unlock John's Gospel. *The back door key is John 20:31.* This key unlocks the whole book. It states the purpose of the Gospel.

The side door key is John 16:28. At the Last Supper with His disciples, Jesus reveals this truth to them: "I came from the Father and entered the world; now I am leaving the world and going back to the Father." He constantly thought that He used to be with the Father. He came down to earth on an errand and stayed for 33 years. He would go back again to His Father.

The front door key is John 1:12. This key hangs right at the very front, outside, low down, within every child's reach: "Yet to all who did receive him, to those who believed in his name, he gave the right to become children of God." This is the great key—the chief key to the whole house. Its use permits the front door to be flung wide open. Anyone who believes may enter.

John

Study Guide:
Understanding the Gospels

In this study, Henrietta Mears urges you to consider the significance of the four accounts of Jesus' life as written by Matthew, Mark, Luke and John. The following questions will help you to understand some of the differences and similarites between these accounts and will highlight what each author was attempting to portray about Jesus in his Gospel.

THE FOUR GOSPELS

1. Why are Matthew, Mark, Luke and John called evangelists?

2. Why would the news about Jesus be thought of as good news?

3. Why are there four Gospels and not just one Gospel?

4. Each Gospel gives us a distinct picture of Jesus. How does each picture help you know Jesus better?

_____

_____

_____

_____

GOD'S PROMISE

A crucial concept in understanding the Gospels is God's promise to His Chosen People, the Jews, to send them a Messiah, or messianic deliverer. Let's examine some of the prominent passages of Scripture along these lines and compare them to various messianic expectations.

5. The word "Messiah" comes from the Hebrew word "to anoint." In the Old Testament, God anointed (i.e., set apart) kings and prophets for special service. The word "Christ" comes from the Greek word also meaning "to anoint." When the New Testament speaks of Jesus Christ, "Christ" is not Jesus' last name; instead, the meaning is "Jesus the Anointed One, the Promised Messiah." Given what we have discovered so far, what would you expect God's anointed Messiah to do (see p. 20)?

_____

_____

_____

_____

6. Read Matthew 3:7-12, which speaks of John the Baptist's confrontation with some religious leaders. When he sees many of the Pharisees and Sadducees coming to where he is baptizing, what does he say?

_____

_____

_____

_____

7. What kind of Messiah was John the Baptist expecting?

_____

_____

_____

_____

8. In 2 Samuel 7:13-14, God makes a promise to King David about the coming Messiah: "He is the one who will build a house for my Name, and I will establish the throne of his kingdom forever. I will be his father, and he will be my son." (This was written about one thousand years before Jesus' birth.) Now read Matthew 22:42. What kind of Messiah were the disciples expecting?

_____

_____

_____

_____

9. Now read Matthew 9:27; 12:23; 15:22. What kind of Messiah were these hurting people expecting?

_____

_____

_____

_____

10. Finally, read Matthew 21:9, which describes Jesus' wild entry into Jerusalem just before He was betrayed and crucified. What kind of Messiah were the common people expecting?

_____

_____

_____

_____

11. In a passage written over seven hundred years before Jesus' birth, Isaiah 53:4-6 says of the coming messianic servant:

Surely he took up our infirmities and carried our sorrows, yet we considered him stricken by God, smitten by him, and afflicted. But he was pierced for our transgressions, he was crushed for our iniquities; the punishment that brought us peace was upon him, and by his wounds we are healed. We all, like sheep, have gone astray, each of us has turned to his own way; and the Lord has laid on him the iniquity of us all.

Compare this passage of Scripture to Matthew 8:16-17. How did Jesus fulfill Isaiah's vision?

_____

_____

_____

_____

12. What does Jesus' fulfillment of Old Testament prophecy say about Him as the Messiah?

_____

_____

_____

_____

_____

13. What does Isaiah 53:4-6 say will be the impact of the death of the Messiah?

_____

_____

_____

_____

_____

_____

14. John 19:34-37 describes the crucifixion scene: "Instead, one of the soldiers pierced Jesus' side with a spear, bringing a sudden flow of blood and water" (verse 34). This piercing of the Messiah is also mentioned in Zechariah 12:10-12. What expectations do these passages convey about the Messiah?

_____

_____

_____

_____

_____

15. Genesis 22:18 is God's irrevocable oath to Abraham that He would follow through on an earlier promise—that "through your offspring all nations on earth will be blessed." Blessing in the Bible includes reconciliation, friendship and fellowship with God. Compare the verses above to Luke 24:45-47. How did Jesus' coming as Messiah fulfill God's promise to Abraham two thousand years earlier?

_____

_____

_____

_____

_____

16. Daniel 7:13-14 identifies an incredible messianic figure. Compare Daniel's vision to what Jesus said about His return in Mark 13:26. According to this verse, how did Jesus describe Himself as Messiah?

_____

_____

_____

_____

_____

17. How accurate do you think all these different expectations are for the coming One who was promised by God? The Bible

actually portrays two comings of the Messiah: the first at a strategic, historical point in time as a servant and Savior, and the second at the end of this present age as a conquering King who brings peace to Earth. Review the various expectations people had for Jesus. Which ones might relate to His first coming? To His second coming?

_____

_____

_____

_____

18. For the sake of argument, let's assume that what the Gospel writers say about Jesus is true and that you believe it is true. How does your belief impact your life?

_____

_____

_____

_____

19. Each Gospel gives us a unique picture of Jesus. With which picture of Jesus do you most identify? Why?

_____

_____

_____

_____

_____

20. How does your picture help you know Jesus better?

_____

_____

_____

_____

_____

Study Guide:
Understanding Matthew

Before you tackle these questions, please spend some time reading the Gospel of Matthew in the Bible.

Nothing is more clear in the Gospel of Matthew than the facts that Matthew was Jewish; he was writing primarily within a Jewish context and community; and Jewish people were his intended audience. Matthew wrote his Gospel to persuade Jewish people that Jesus was the Messiah who was promised in the Hebrew Bible (i.e., the Old Testament—the Jewish Scriptures).

COMING OF THE KING (MATTHEW 1–2)

1. How would the following Scripture passages have connected with Matthew's Jewish readers?

   Matthew 1:1, which states: "A record of the *genealogy* of Jesus Christ the *son of David,* the *son of Abraham* (emphasis added). (Hint: Regarding "genealogy," quickly scan 1 Chronicles 1–9 and think about how important ancestry and bloodlines were in Jewish culture. Regarding "son of David," see "Understanding the Gospels," study question 8. Regarding "son of Abraham," review Henrietta Mears's commentary under "Matthew 1–2: Birth of the King.")

   _____

   _____

   _____

   _____

   _____

Matthew 1:18-23, which depicts the moral dilemma facing Joseph—betrothed to a pregnant Mary—given the Jewish religious, social and cultural norms of the time.

_____

_____

_____

_____

_____

Matthew 1:22-23; 2:5-6,14-15,17-18,23; 3:3,15 (and many other places in Matthew's Gospel), which fulfill the prophecies of events surrounding Jesus' purpose, deeds and career.

_____

_____

_____

_____

Matthew 2:1, which states that "Jesus was born in Bethlehem in Judea, during the time of King Herod." (Hint: Compare to 2 Kings 18:13; 24:1; Ezra 4:6—passages in which God-events important in Jewish history are anchored to secular history. How is God's participation in human history different from non-biblical views of God that portray Him as aloof from human affairs or as an abstract an impersonal "higher power.")

_____

_____

_____

_____

_____

Matthew 6:24 and 22:37, which reveal the basic assumption that there is one true God who deserves all worship, as opposed to other religions and worldviews that embrace many gods and spirits. (Compare with Deuteronomy 6:4-5 and Exodus 20:3.)

_____

_____

_____

_____

FINDING TRUTH

Many people seek to create God in their own image and likeness. Ignoring the historical and cultural context Jesus lived in, they miss the intended messages coming out of that context.

A classic example of this tendency occurred in the 1930s when many German "Christians" bought hook, line and sinker the Nazi Aryan indoctrination that made Jesus into a virtual non-Jew and denigrated everything Jewish.

2. Can you think of any contemporary examples of people who ignore Jesus' Jewishness and message and mold Him into an expression of their own religion or worldview? (Hint: Jesus as an "ascended master," or Jesus as a social reformer.)

_____

_____

_____

_____

3. How does the historical setting and context of Jesus' message help us see the truth of His words and deeds?

_____

_____

_____

_____

Study Guide

PROCLAMATION OF THE KINGDOM
(MATTHEW 3–16:20)

Jesus' famous Sermon on the Mount (see Matthew 5–7) is universally regarded as the most profound encapsulation of moral teaching in the Bible. Let's dig a little deeper into this mountain of spiritual truth.

4. Read the Beatitudes (see Matthew 5:3-12). Reflect on the meaning of each one. How are you doing on your poverty of spirit (admitting a desperate need for spiritual help from God), your meekness (controlling your strength according to God's direction), your hunger and thirst for righteousness (as opposed to desiring entertainment or making more money) and your identifying with Christ despite public mockery and insults?

   _____

   _____

   _____

   _____

5. Take a look at Matthew 5:21-22,27-29. Jesus moves morality from mere behavior to the motives and thoughts of the heart. What is Jesus trying to teach us?

   _____

   _____

   _____

   _____

6. Notice Jesus' teaching on forgiveness in Matthew 6:12,14-15. According to Jesus, what are the consequences if you hold grudges and are unwilling forgive others?

   _____

   _____

   _____

   _____

7. Matthew 7:12 says, "So in everything, do to others what you would have them do to you, for this sums up the Law and the Prophets." How is the attitude with which we treat others part of God's plan (see Matthew 5:3)?

_____

_____

_____

_____

_____

8. An important aspect of Jesus' ethical teaching is found in Matthew 23:23. According to Jesus, *all* of Scripture is God's Word, and *all* will be fulfilled (see Matthew 5:17-18); therefore, there are such things as moral absolutes. Yet here Jesus clearly acknowledges that *some* matters of the Law are *weightier* or more important than others. What are these weightier matters?

_____

_____

_____

_____

_____

Witnessing Miracles

Jesus' proclamation of God's kingdom was accompanied by miracles, and we have plenty of them in Matthew 8–9.

9. What do you notice about the crowd's reactions to Jesus' miracles? Why would some people be apprehensive or angered by what Jesus did?

_____

_____

_____

_____

_____

10. How would Jesus' miracles enhance His proclamation of the kingdom of God being "at hand" (see Matthew 4:17, *KJV*)?

_____

_____

_____

_____

Identifying with Christ

One of the most beautiful things about the Gospels is how they invite us into a discipleship relationship with Jesus, just like Jesus' 12 disciples had.

11. What hope do you take from the fact that the disciples Jesus chose were not the high and mighty ones in society?

_____

_____

_____

_____

12. Reread Matthew 10:32-33. According to Jesus, how important is it for Christians to publicly identify themselves with Christ? Why do you think this identification is so important to Jesus?

_____

_____

_____

_____

REJECTION OF THE KING
(MATTHEW 16:21–20)

The previous question leads directly to what Henrietta Mears calls "Life's Most Important Question" and "Life's Most Important Answer" (see p. 43).

13. What have you done personally with Jesus Christ? "Have you," as Mears asks, "put Christ on the throne of your life?" What would it mean to you if you took this step?

_____

_____

_____

_____

14. What does "become a Christian" mean? Is becoming a Christian just a matter of raising your hand at an evangelistic meeting? Or is it a matter of Christ profoundly altering you? How does Jesus taking up residence in your life make a difference in you? (Read "Becoming a Member of God's Family" on pp. 169-172 for help and ideas.)

_____

_____

_____

_____

THE FUTURE OF THE KINGDOM (24–25)

15. Read Matthew's description of Jesus' sufferings for us on the cross in Matthew 27:32-50. Reflect on what Jesus did for you, personally. What does it mean to you that Jesus endured the cross on your behalf?

_____

_____

_____

_____

16. Matthew portrays Jesus not just as the promised Jewish Messiah but also as the Savior of the world. Turn to Matthew 28:18-20. Here, the resurrected Christ gives His disciples the

Great Commission. Read is each phrase of the Great Commission below.

Jesus first says, "All authority in heaven and on earth has been given to me" (verse 18). What type of person would say this kind of thing if it were not true? As the true Savior of the world, what do these words say about Jesus?

_____

_____

_____

_____

_____

Jesus then says, "Therefore go and make disciples of all nations . . . teaching them to obey everything I have commanded you" (verses 19-20). The phrase "all nations" means all the ethnic or people groups of the world. According to this passage, what was Jesus' plan for the kingdom of God? What impact would the Kingdom have on the cultures of the world?

_____

_____

_____

_____

_____

Jesus adds, "Baptizing them in the name of the Father and of the Son and of the Holy Spirit" (verse 19). The Father, Son and Holy Spirit are the three ways our great God reveals Himself to us. This three-in-one idea is called the Trinity. Being baptized is a way to publicly show that you belong to Jesus. Why is this step important to your life as a follower of Christ?

_____

_____

_____

_____

Jesus concludes, "And surely I am with you always, to the very end of the age" (verse 20). This promise is amazing. Jesus says that He will personally be with each and every one of His followers "always." Never again do we have to feel alone, because Jesus is here. Since Jesus really is in the here and now, what would you like to say to Him? Say it silently or say it out loud; it doesn't matter. But say something from your heart.

_____

_____

_____

_____

_____

17. How does Matthew's picture of Jesus as our king impact how you see Him?

_____

_____

_____

_____

_____

18. What does it mean to be a disciple of Jesus?

_____

_____

_____

_____

_____

19. What do people learn about Jesus when they look at your life?

_____

_____

_____

_____

Study Guide

20. Read Matthew 28:16-20. How does Matthew close his Gospel? What instructions does Jesus give to His followers?

_____

_____

_____

_____

_____

21. What are you doing to fulfill this commandment in your present situation?

_____

_____

_____

_____

_____

22. How can you more clearly represent Christ to others?

_____

_____

_____

_____

_____

23. How does knowing Jesus is with you always help you obey Him and share Him with others?

_____

_____

_____

_____

_____

_____

Study Guide: Understanding Mark

Whereas Matthew's Gospel was crafted particularly for a Jewish audience, Mark's Gospel was designed to reach the Romans, or people dominated by Roman culture and thinking. The Romans were non-Jews—aware of Jewish culture and religion, and had dealings with Jewish people, but not necessarily familiar with all things Jewish. Mark, whose message is just as universal as Matthew's (see Matthew 28:18-20), makes a special effort to make the gospel of Jesus understandable to the Romans. Let's put this into context.

1. The Romans promoted a certain amount of tolerance for religions, even though they also promoted emperor worship and supremacy of the Roman state. Read Mark 1:1,15. Why do you think Mark's mention of Jesus as the Son of God and the kingdom of God as being "at hand" would have gotten the attention of Roman readers?

_____

_____

_____

_____

2. The Romans valued *pietas* (duty), *gravitas* (seriousness of purpose) and *dignitas* (a sense of personal worth). Why would a Roman audience be more interested in what Jesus did than what He claimed to be (see pp. 50-51)?

_____

_____

_____

3. The Romans thought they were above what they perceived as narrow-mindedness. Read Mark 2:23–3:6, which describes Jesus' treatment of the Sabbath. What principles did Jesus use to supercede the Pharisee's idea of keeping the Sabbath? What reactions might a Roman reader have had to this story?

_____

_____

_____

4. The Romans would likely have been baffled by the intricacies of Jewish traditions about what was religiously clean and unclean. Read Mark 7:1-23. What does Mark say to help his Roman readers understand the issues at stake? (Hint: Read verses 14-23; see also verses 3-4).

_____

_____

_____

_____

Read again these other passages, which Mark wrote to help his readers who are unfamiliar with Jewish language and customs: 3:17; 5:41; 7:34; 15:16,22,34,42.

5. Among the Romans were many God fearers (see Acts 10:2). These were people fed up with the mythologies and superstitions of polytheistic religion and were attracted to the purity of monotheism as taught in Judaism. They might have visited a synagogue, but they weren't ready to convert to Judaism. What might a typical God-fearer have thought of Mark 12:28-34?

_____

_____

_____

_____

Study Guide

THE LORD AS KING AND SERVANT

While a major theme of Matthew's Gospel is the kingdom of God, with Jesus as the messianic King, Mark's Gospel abundantly emphasizes Jesus as the servant of God.

6. Think about kings, queens and monarchies in two opposing ways: (1) what attracts us; and (2) what repels us?

_____
_____
_____
_____
_____

7. Now think through Jesus' career on Earth as presented by Matthew and Mark. How is Jesus like a king; and how does He break with kingly stereotypes? (Hint: Mears provides a lot of examples.)

_____
_____
_____
_____
_____
_____

THE SERVANT PREPARED (MARK 1:1-13)

Henrietta Mears does something very interesting in the next two sections. She likens Jesus' human life to ours.

8. Reflecting on how God prepared Jesus for His life's work, Mears says, "Preparation in life is always needed. . . . Getting ready for our life's work is of tremendous importance. Don't

become impatient if Christ uses time to prepare you for life"
(pp. 53-54). How can you bring Christ into your preparation
for your life's work today?

_____

_____

_____

_____

9. Reflecting on the oddness of John the Baptist, Mears says,
   "There is a lesson here for us. God does not always choose the
   kind of person we would select. He often picks 'the foolish
   things of the world to shame the wise . . . the weak things of
   the world to shame the strong' (1 Corinthians 1:27)" (p. 54).
   How often have you written yourself off as someone too odd
   for God to use significantly? How often have you written oth-
   ers off that way?

_____

_____

_____

_____

10. What can you do right now to again put your life in His hands,
    at His disposal? What can you say to ask Him to help you see
    the potential in others?

_____

_____

_____

_____

_____

11. Reflecting on John's message of repentance, Mears says, "A
    true revival is always a revival of righteousness" (p. 54). Re-
    vivals are a mixture of human and divine elements. A revival

is true when people are awakened to God's reality through Christ, and their lives are transformed by that experience. A false revival is when people go through the motions but aren't really changed. For Christians who really want to walk with Christ, how does a revival of righteousness begin?

_____

_____

_____

_____

_____

_____

_____

Reflecting on the temptation of Christ, Henrietta Mears says, "Suffering and trials are as much God's plan as thrills and triumphs" (p. 56). Let that sink in a while. It's not often preached as straight as that, but it's as true for Jesus as it is for you. Pray this thought back to the Lord. Henrietta Mears also says some remarkable things based upon the Scriptures:

- "Jesus was 'sent' to be tempted. It was no accident or evil fate but a divine appointment."

- "Temptation has its place in this world. We would never develop without it."

- "There is nothing wrong in being tempted. The wrong begins when we consent to it."

- "We will find that the path of duty often takes us through temptations."

- "He always makes a way of escape [from temptation]!"

Meditate on each of these thoughts, and apply each of them to your own life. Repent as needed. Then memorize and meditate on 1 Corinthians 10:13.

THE SERVANT WORKING (MARK 1:14–8:30)

Henrietta Mears's discussion continues as she likens Jesus' human life to ours.

12. Reflecting on Jesus' calling of fishermen to follow Him and become "fishers of men," Mears says, "It is interesting to note that Jesus never called any idle person" (p. 57). This is vintage Henrietta Mears. She advocated the strenuous life and lived unabashedly for the Lord Jesus Christ. How are you fully engaged in the great gift of life?

_____

_____

_____

_____

_____

13. Reflecting on the phrase "at once they left their nets and followed him" (Mark 1:18), Mears says, "Too often there is time lost between our call and our coming; our doing lags far behind our duty" (p. 57). In what ways have you tried to put God on hold rather than quickly obeying Him or following His lead in your life?

_____

_____

_____

_____

_____

_____

Study Guide

14. Reflecting on the fact that Jesus made time to get away from the crowds and pray alone with God, Mears says, "If the Son of God needed to pray before He undertook His work, how much more should we pray? Perhaps if we lack success in life, it is because we fail to pray. In other words, we have not because we ask not (see James 4:2)" (p. 60). How is prayer part

of your preparation for each day? What can you do to set up a regular, daily habit of bringing your concerns to God?

_____

_____

_____

_____

_____

15. One passage that forever establishes Jesus' unique claim to deity is Mark 2:1-11. Jesus, the servant of God, heals the paralytic man, which proves His healing power and authority from God for spiritual healing from sin. The most disarming thing you can say to someone about your Christian faith is "Jesus died for sinners like me." How do you see yourself in this statement? How could you share this concept with someone else?

_____

_____

_____

_____

_____

16. Reflecting on Jesus' choice of the 12 apostles in Mark 3, Mears focuses on the phrase "that they might be with him" (verse 14). She says, "Mark it in your Bible" (p. 60). So get your Bible out and do it now! Why is it important for Christians to be with Christ every moment of every day?

_____

_____

_____

_____

_____

Reflecting on how Jesus gathered His followers together after their first missionary journey (see Mark 6:30), Mears says, "No Christian work can be carried on for any length of time without frequent talks with Christ. We need His sympathy, approval, guidance and strength" (p. 63). Do you see what Mark's Gospel is teaching us? As it was for the disciples, so it is for us. Take some time now to seek Jesus' sympathy, approval, guidance and strength. He's waiting for you right now.

THE SERVANT REJECTED (MARK 8:31–15)

17. Mark 11:15–12:36 shows Jesus trying to persuade the Jews to receive Him as the Messiah. How do they respond? What warning did Jesus give about following the teachers of the Law (see 12:36-40)?

_____

_____

_____

_____

18. The Jewish authorities rejected Jesus as their Messiah. Why do people reject Jesus today?

_____

_____

_____

_____

19. What purpose did Christ's suffering serve?

_____

_____

_____

20. Henrietta Mears says regarding Mark 11:15–12:44 that "Jesus sought to persuade the Jews to receive Him as the Messiah" (p. 65). For generations Jewish leaders have tried to

persuade the public that being Jewish and believing in Jesus are incompatible. Yet in Jesus' time, some Jews did believe in Him. The same is true today—there are some Jews who believe in Jesus, many of them now worshiping in messianic synagogues. What are some challenges that you think Jews today face in accepting Jesus? What insight or advantages might a Jewish believer have over non-Jewish believers?

----

21. Henrietta Mears, reflecting on the attacks of Jesus' enemies that led to His death, says, "All the way through, the perfect servant of God was dogged by His enemies" (p. 67). What enemy or enemies exist today? What expectation should Christians have about opposition to the gospel?

THE SERVANT EXALTED (MARK 16)

Reflecting on the two versions of the Great Commission in Matthew and Mark, Mears says, "In Mark we see in Jesus' words that His disciples are to take His place, and He will serve in and through them. He is still the servant, though risen (see Mark 16:20). The command for service resounds with urgency. Not a corner of the world is to be left unvisited, not a soul to be left out!" (pp. 66–67).

22. How do obeying, following and supporting the Great Commission express love?

_____

_____

_____

_____

_____

23. How does failure to obey, follow and support the Great Commission express lack of love?

_____

_____

_____

_____

_____

24. Mark 10:45 says, "For even the Son of Man did not come to be served, but to serve, and to give his life as a ransom for many." Even though Mark's Gospel emphasizes Jesus as the servant of God, look at how Jesus finishes in Mark 16:19: "After the Lord Jesus had spoken to them, he was taken up into heaven and he sat at the right hand of God." The phrase "right hand" of God occurs throughout the New Testament (see Matthew 22:44; Mark 12:36; 14:62; Luke 20:42; 22:69; Acts 2:25,33-34; 5:31; 7:55-56; Romans 8:34; Ephesians 1:20; Colossians 3:1; Hebrews 1:3,13; 8:1; 10:12; 12:2; 1 Peter 3:22). It is a staple of New Testament preaching and teaching. Look up these verses and verify for yourself the overriding importance of this fact of Christian faith. Can you think of any implications for your own life from this stupendous fact?

_____

_____

_____

_____

_____

POINTS TO REMEMBER

In this section, Henrietta Mears continues to bring home the implications of Mark's Gospel. Reflecting on the plot that led to Jesus' death (see Mark 14:1), Mears reminds us that the message of Jesus is like a sword that divides: "The greatest sin of this age, as of every age, is the rejection of Jesus Christ. . . . The people of Jesus' day made their choice, and the people of our day must make theirs" (p. 68).

25. Do you agree that the greatest sin is to reject Jesus Christ? Why or why not?

_____

_____

_____

_____

26. Mears says, "Everyone who has heard the gospel must either accept the Lord as Savior or reject Him" (p. 68). How does Mark develop this theme?

_____

_____

_____

_____

27. How does this challenge compare to the following attitudes?

A lifelong churchgoer says, "Jesus was totally nonjudgmental and would never do anything to make people feel guilty."

_____

_____

_____

_____

Study Guide

A church member asks, "Do you believe in the Lordship of Christ?" His minister answers, "It's not for me to tell God how to be God."

_____

_____

_____

_____

_____

28. It is vogue among some churchgoers today to say the essence of the gospel is "inclusiveness." Would Mark and Henrietta Mears agree?

_____

_____

_____

_____

_____

29. In what ways is the gospel inclusive (i.e., for all peoples)? In what ways is the gospel exclusive (i.e., not for everyone)?

_____

_____

_____

_____

_____

_____

30. If the gospel of Jesus is a message that requires people to admit they need a Savior rather than to persist in self-sufficiency, how will the message of Jesus ever continue to divide people?

_____

_____

_____

_____

_____

Study Guide:
Understanding Luke

If Matthew's audience was primarily Jewish people, and Mark's was Romans, who was Luke thinking of as he wrote?

Henrietta Mears mentions that Luke's intended audience was the Greeks and other people greatly influenced by Hellenistic culture and values. This can be a bit confusing, because a great deal of cultural accommodation, borrowing and intertwining was happening at the time. The prevailing culture in the Roman Empire was actually a Greco-Roman stew.

1. Studies of Greek mythology often focus on the ideal of human perfection and beauty. What Greek hero or god can you recall who truly embodied full perfection?

   _____

   _____

   _____

2. Greek art and drama examined the depths of human emotions and often played on the disparity between the nobility of man and his foolishness, pettiness and cruelty. Mears says that Luke "reveals the Savior as a man with all His sympathies, feelings and growing powers—a Savior suited to all" (pp. 72-73). Read Hebrews 2:5-18 for a poignant summary of how Jesus was made like us to bring us to God. What did the Son of God give up to become a man?

   _____

   _____

   _____

   _____

3. Jesus was unlike us in one very important aspect, and Henrietta Mears boils this down to one significant word—"holy" (p. 73). Another way of saying this is found in Hebrews 4:15, which says Jesus "was without sin." This is in contrast to 1 John 1:8, which says, "If we claim to be without sin, we deceive ourselves and the truth is not in us." How can sinful people have a relationship with a holy God?

_____

_____

_____

_____

_____

_____

4. Mears says, "Christ, the creator of this universe, entered this world like any other person" (p. 73). As amazing as it sounds, this is the clear testimony of Scripture. See John 1:1-3,14 and Colossians 1:15-17. When the Bible declares God made the heavens and the earth, the Son of God was intimately involved. The universe was made "by him and for him" (Colossians 1:16). Who fashioned you and gave you life? Who sustains you every moment of your life? To whom do you owe your life?

_____

_____

_____

_____

_____

_____

5. The Bible teaches that God has always existed as God the Father, God the Son and God the Holy Spirit. The Incarnation is the teaching that God the Son took upon Himself human flesh and dwelt among us in order to make it possible to bring us back to God. Read Psalm 113. Has God ever been an

aloof, far-off God? How does Psalm 113 anticipate what Jesus did for us?

-----

6. If Jesus grew up like us—toiled with His hands, laughed, wept and prayed—how does that help us as we pray?

-----

7. The Bible teaches that Jesus grew up like us. Mears says, "There was no mention of unhealthy or supernatural growth" (p. 73). What she means is that Jesus had a normal childhood. The authentic Gospels resist the temptation to embellish the record with giddy speculations. By contrast, some spurious gospels create fantastic and weird stories of Jesus' supposed miraculous powers as a child—in one He is supposed to have blown onto clay pigeons and made them alive! How would these stories diminish the authentic Gospels' representation of Jesus?

-----

8. One profound result of the Incarnation is how it affirms the human dignity of all people. Mears says, "Luke is the Gospel for the outcast on the earth" (p. 74). Then she talks about Luke's unique attitude toward women—an attitude that contrasted sharply with cultural attitudes toward women then and even now. Have you ever felt like an outcast? Can you

imagine how women or lepers felt when they were rejected or put down by society? How did Jesus raise up the outcasts?

9. The profound truth of the intrinsic worth of individuals extends past the boundaries of the people of Israel. In Jewish tradition, the Gentiles (non-Jews) were seen as not only far from God (which was true) but also unloved by God (which is not what the Scriptures teach). According to Mears, what was one of the hardest lessons for the Early Church (which at first was primarily Jewish) to learn (see pp. 74-75)? Why?

10. Was Jesus' ministry only to Jews, or was it also directed toward Gentiles?

THE PREPARATION OF THE SON OF MAN
(LUKE 1:1–4:13)

11. Luke shows how God used people to accomplish His plan. How is this evident in the circumstances of Jesus' birth? In His baptism? In His lineage?

12. After Jesus' temptation by the devil in the wilderness, Mears gives us some pertinent spiritual application: "As Jesus came forth from the fire of testing in the unquenchable 'power of the Spirit,' so too can we. Only as we are filled with His Spirit can we overcome temptation" (p. 80). Do you think the "unquenchable 'power of the Spirit'" is only for super-Christians or for all Christians? Why?

_____

_____

_____

_____

13. Besides enabling us to overcome temptation, what does it mean to be filled with "the unquenchable 'power of the Spirit'"?

_____

_____

_____

_____

14. Is being filled with the unquenchable power of the Holy Spirit something that Christians should avoid or eagerly seek? Why?

_____

_____

_____

_____

THE MINISTRY OF THE SON OF MAN
(LUKE 4:14–19)

15. In this section, we are introduced to Jesus' divine mission. We see that Jesus was brought up in a godly home. He was accustomed to going to synagogue on the day of worship. What is

the impact of building a godly home? What can you do to invite or strengthen God's presence in your home?

16. In Luke 4:18-19, Jesus quotes from Isaiah 61:1-2, which was a way of referencing all the promises God had made to His people. Read Isaiah 61:1-2. Notice that Jesus omitted the last phrase of Isaiah 61:2 in His reading. What does this tell you about Jesus' mission?

17. How does Luke 4:18-19 describe what happens when the Spirit of the Lord is upon His servant?

18. Henrietta Mears says that Jesus "is our Kinsman-Redeemer" (p. 83). This phrase comes from Ruth 3:9; 4:14. A Kinsman-Redeemer was a close relative who had the right and the means to buy another out of slavery or debt. How has Jesus been a Kinsman-Redeemer for you?

19. Jesus anticipated that the people in His hometown would re-
sist His message. He actually provoked them to reveal their
hearts when He said that just as people did not believe the
Old Testament prophets, so they also would have difficulty
believing in Him. Jesus recounts an incident in which Elijah
was sent to a Sidonian woman's house (a non-Jew). He also
says that Naaman the Syrian (a non-Jew) was cleansed of his
leprosy in the time of Elisha. How would these examples have
gone against the expectations of the townspeople?

_____

_____

_____

_____

_____

20. Why would they have wanted to throw Jesus off a cliff? (Hint:
See what Henrietta Mears says under "A Gospel for the
World" [see p. 83].)

_____

_____

_____

_____

_____

21. Read Romans 1:16. Is there any indication in this verse that
the gospel—God's Word—is just one of the religions of the
world and that all of the world's religions are equal?

_____

_____

_____

_____

_____

Study Guide

22. Jesus pursued relationships with "tax collectors and sinners" (Luke 7:34). What was Jesus' goal for these relationships (see Luke 19:10)?

_____

_____

_____

_____

23. Jesus also invested in training those who followed Him. What was His goal for these relationship (see pp. 84-86)?

_____

_____

_____

_____

_____

THE SUFFERING OF THE SON OF MAN
(LUKE 20:1–23:56)

Henrietta Mears takes us on an almost eyewitness tour of the last hours of Jesus' life. Periodically reflecting on Jesus' last days is something that all Christians need to do, soberly and reverently. The reason Jesus instituted the Last Supper is so that we would perpetually remember the cross until He comes again.

24. Read the Scripture passages in this section of Luke and try to imagine yourself in the moment, feeling everything: the weather, the nonverbal communication, the tones of voice, the tiredness, the layers of betrayal and abandonment, the prayers, the sweat, the blood, the wood and the iron. Henrietta Mears says the thief on the cross "was saved . . . the way every sinner must be saved" (p. 87). What way is that?

_____

_____

_____

_____

THE VICTORY OF THE SON OF MAN (LUKE 24)

The first thing this section recounts is the story of the walk to Emmaus. The resurrected Christ walks with two disciples down the road to Emmaus, but they don't recognize Him. The key verse is Luke 24:26, *NASB*: "Was it not *necessary* for the Christ to suffer these things and to enter into His glory?" (emphasis added).

25. A lot of people think the sacrifice of Christ on the cross for the sins of humanity was unnecessary and even barbaric. But according to Jesus, it was both *predicted* and *necessary*! Verse 27 says: "And beginning with Moses and all the Prophets, he explained to them what was said in all the Scriptures concerning himself." In Jewish tradition, "beginning with Moses" includes the first five books of the Bible attributed to Moses. "All the Prophets" indicates prophetic history from Joshua—where Moses' writing left off—to Malachi—the last book in the Bible. In other words, *Jesus was saying the whole Hebrew Bible pointed toward Himself!* The Messiah's coming wasn't an afterthought—Jesus' coming is the purpose of history! What does this tell us about God's love for us?

    ----

26. Which Old Testament Scriptures do you think might point to Jesus, either in direct prophecies or in archetypes, symbols, tokens, signs, distinguishing characteristics, models, patterns, foreshadows or forms (see Genesis 22:1-18; Exodus 12; Deuteronomy 18:18; Psalms 2; 16:9-11; 22; 110; Isaiah 53)?

    ----

27. Why might people be offended by the idea that the atonement (i.e., Jesus' sacrifice for us) was necessary?

_____

_____

_____

_____

28. Why do you think Jesus thought it was necessary to die on the cross? What does the need for Jesus' sacrifice tell us about the seriousness of our sin?

_____

_____

_____

_____

29. Notice what happens to the men: "Were not our hearts burning within us while he talked with us on the road and opened the Scriptures to us?" (verse 32). How do you react to this revelation about Christ in the Old Testament? Are you kind of blasé about it, or does it really fire you up? Why?

_____

_____

_____

_____

30 The physical resurrection of Christ is a bedrock belief of Christian faith. In fact, the apostle Paul says in 1 Corinthians 15:14: "If Christ has not been raised, our preaching is useless and so is your faith," and we might as well "eat and drink, for tomorrow we die" (15:32). On what basis might people dismiss the Christian claim of the resurrection of Christ? Does it really matter if Christ was raised or not? Why or why not?

_____

_____

_____

Study Guide:
Understanding John

Before beginning this study of the Gospel of John, it is impor-
tant to understand some Old Testament concepts about God,
how John's Gospel relates to those concepts and Henrietta Mears's
commentary on them.

The book of Exodus depicts God leading the Israelites out of
Egypt with miracles and wonders. Moses regularly pauses and
asks the Lord for guidance at what he calls "the tent of meeting"
(Exodus 33:7). On one occasion the Lord promises, "My Presence
will go with you" (33:14). Then Moses boldly asks, "Show me your
glory" (verse 18).

The Lord replies, " 'I will cause all my goodness to pass in front
of you, and I will proclaim my name, the Lord, in your presence.
I will have mercy on whom I will have mercy, and I will have com-
passion on whom I have compassion. But,' he said, 'you cannot
see my face, for no one may see me and live' " (verses 19-20).

1. Why would coming face-to-face with God have been such an
   awesome, holy, terrifying and dangerous experience?

   ....

   ....

   ....

   ....

   ....

   ....

2. The following are other passages in the Old Testament that
   describe people seeing God. Look these verses up and then
   write down what these episodes have in common.

Genesis 32:24-30: Jacob wrestles with God.

_____

_____

_____

_____

_____

Exodus 3:6: God spoke to Moses at the burning bush.

_____

_____

_____

_____

Exodus 24:9-11: The 70 elders eat and drink before God.

_____

_____

_____

_____

Judges 6:22-23: Gideon sees the angel of the Lord face-to-face.

_____

_____

_____

_____

Judges 13:22: Manoah sees the angel of the Lord.

_____

_____

_____

_____

3. The above passages are the background to John 1:18. Refer-
   ring to this verse, Henrietta Mears says, "No person could see
   God" (p. 98). Read John 1:18. What is unique about Jesus

compared to God the Father, whom Old Testament believers saw in some powerful, life-threatening and life-transforming way but did not die?

---

4. The Old Testament says the beginning of wisdom is the fear of the Lord (see Proverbs 1:7). How does Exodus 33:20 relate to the fear, reverence and respect for God we see in the Bible? What do these Old Testament passages suggest about undue familiarity with the awesome, holy God?

---

5. Read John 1:17. Moses was and remains the most prominent human figure in all of Judaism. Why? How does John compare Jesus with Moses? What is Jesus able to do that Moses could not?

Mears mentions that John's Gospel was written after the fateful events of AD 70. Titus, the Roman general, utterly destroyed Jerusalem and its Temple after a horrible siege. Titus also banished the Jewish people from Jerusalem and its environs. The significance of this military defeat had huge consequences for the history of the Jewish people.

The reason for the great loss is that before AD 70, Judaism had been a Temple religion. Every morning and evening animal sacrifices were made for sins small and large. The Temple was the center of community, religious, civil and political life. Festivals were held at the Temple. We must remember that Herod's Temple—called by Jewish historians the Second Temple (the first was Solomon's Temple)—was a bona fide wonder of the ancient world. The people had great pride in the Temple—the center of their lives.

6. After AD 70, the Jews were decimated. Without the Temple, sacrifices, the priesthood (ancestral records having been destroyed) and their main city—and forbidden to enter or come near their once glorious city—they were left hopeless and mourned the thousands dead. Try to imagine what a devastating blow this was. What impact might this event have had on the Early Church members, many of whom were Jewish believers in Jesus? What impact might it have had on John himself?

   _____

   _____

   _____

   _____

7. Read Matthew 24:2 and Luke 19:44. Jesus actually predicted in graphic terms this very defeat. He foresaw the end of the sacrificial system and the ruin of the beautiful Temple. The New Testament book of Hebrews (written before AD 70) follows Jesus' lead, anticipating the disappearance of the Old Covenant and the old sacrificial system. Read Hebrews 8:13 and Hebrews 10. Why does the author of Hebrews say this would happen?

   _____

   _____

   _____

   _____

8. John's Gospel does not mention the events of AD 70 directly, but as you read, there are hints of the implications of the fall of Jerusalem and the destruction of the Temple. For example, John is the first Gospel writer to mention that John the Bap-

tist (a different John than the author of John's Gospel) had very early called Jesus "the Lamb of God, who takes away the sin of the world!" (1:29). Given the Temple sacrifices and the yearly Passover festival in which many lambs were sacrificed, what might the Jews have thought about this declaration?

_____

_____

_____

_____

JESUS' DEITY

Mears mentions, "In these days of widespread departure from the truth, the deity of Christ Jesus must be emphasized" (p. 92). If this was true in the past, it is certainly more true today. Listen to the words of John S. Spong, an Episcopal bishop of New Jersey—a man who at one time actually took vows to defend the Christian faith! After he denied that we can believe in a theistic God (i.e., God is maker of heaven and Earth), Spong says:

> It is nonsensical to seek to understand Jesus as the incarnation of the theistic deity. So the Christology of the ages is bankrupt. The virgin birth, understood as literal biology, makes Christ's divinity, as traditionally understood, impossible. The view of the cross as the sacrifice for the sins of the world is a barbarian idea based on primitive concepts of God and must be dismissed.[1]

9. John Spong may be a very charming, charismatic, intelligent fellow. But if denials of core Christian truths like this are coming *from church leaders within the churches,* what can you do to be on your guard against such false teachers?

_____

_____

_____

_____

10. Review the list of ways that Jesus' diety is portrayed through-out John (see pp. 93-94). What is your response to those who object to the deity of Christ by saying that Jesus never claimed to be God?

_____

_____

_____

_____

_____

THE GREAT PROLOGUE (JOHN 1:1-18)

The great prologue is one of the most important passages in the whole Bible. Read John 1:1-18 in its entirety.

11. What is significant to you about the great prologue? What jumps out at you?

_____

_____

_____

_____

_____

12. Henrietta Mears mentions that John 1:1-18 "opens like the book of Genesis" (p. 97). How does John 1 open like Genesis 1? What are some word and thought parallels?

_____

_____

_____

_____

_____

13. What happens when God speaks the word in Genesis 1? How might God's Word in Genesis be related to Jesus, the Word of God, in John 1 (see also Colossians 1:16 and Hebrews 1:2)?

_____

_____

_____

_____

14. In Genesis 1, God's Word perfectly expresses God's personal will. How might Jesus, the Word of God, also fulfill that role (see John 1:14,18)?

_____

_____

_____

_____

15. There are various ways the term "Word of God" is used in the Bible. The Word of God (or Word of the Lord) may be revealed to a prophet of God; the Old Testament as a whole may be called the Word of God; the New Testament preaching of the gospel or revelation of truth can be called the Word of God; and here in John's Gospel Jesus Himself is called the Word of God. What is similar and what is different about these various uses of the term? If Jesus is the Word behind all these other true words of God, what ought to be your response to hearing the Word of God?

_____

_____

_____

_____

16. Some religious teachers at the time of John were happy to talk eloquently about God's Word but were offended by the idea that the Word would sully itself by taking on flesh. They believed that spirit was good and flesh was evil, promoting the

idea that the spirit of man was imprisoned in the prison-house of the body. Read John 1:14 and 1 John 4:2 (a short letter also written by John). How would John have responded to these false teachers' feelings?

_____

_____

_____

_____

All of the titles we get for Jesus from this great prologue are remarkable. Mears mentions: "truly God, light of life, declarer of God the Father, baptizer with the Holy Spirit" (p. 97). Is Jesus your true God? Is He the light of your life? Has He declared God's goodness to you? Has He baptized you with the Holy Spirit? If you're not sure, ask Him to be these things to you right now!

The Son of Man

Mears explains that "Christ became what He was not previously— a man [at the Incarnation]. But Christ did not cease to be God. He was God-Man" (p. 97). This concept must be accepted by faith; it will not ever be adequately understood. The disciples at first experienced Jesus as a man; but through His character, miracles, teaching and finally, His death and resurrection, they gradually came to understand who He really was.

17. You now have seen what the Bible clearly teaches about Jesus. Do you personally think He was just another prophet, like Unitarianism and Islam teach, or do you believe He is the unique Son of God? Do you think it is legitimate to put Christ alongside religious teachers like Muhammad and Buddha, or is Christ totally unique in all of history? Why?

_____

_____

_____

_____

Study Guide

18. Genesis 1:26 actually means that humans have rational, spiritual, relational, creative and moral capacities that reflect God Himself. Therefore, all people—even the weak, the poor and the outcasts—have intrinsic worth and dignity. When we sin, we not only act against God, but we also act against what it means to be truly human (i.e., created in God's image). We violate our human dignity. Henrietta Mears says, "People had sinned and no longer reflected the image of God, so Christ— 'the image of the invisible God' (Colossians 1:15)—came to dwell with people" (p. 98). In your life today, how can the living Christ more fully restore the image of God (lost through sin) in you?

Placing Our Faith in Jesus

Mears quotes the paradoxical statement of John 1:11: "He came to that which was his own [i.e., the Jewish people], but his own did not receive him" (p. 98). This is actually an overstatement, since we know many of "his own" did put their trust in Jesus:

- The 12 apostles, the women who followed Him and many in the crowds believed in Jesus.
- Nicodemus (see John 3:1-8; 7:50-52) and Joseph of Arimathea (see 19:38-42)—two leading Jewish figures in Jerusalem—believed in Jesus.
- "Many even among the leaders believed in him," according to John 12:42.
- For the first two decades of the Jesus Movement, almost all of His followers were Jewish!

However, belief in Jesus and confessing Him as Lord are sometimes complex.

19. Isaiah 6:9-10 is quoted in all four Gospels (see Matthew 13:14-15; Mark 4:12; Luke 8:10; John 12:40-41). Isaiah wrote about 750 years before Christ. What complaint did he have against the future generation that would largely reject the Messiah?

20. Read John 12:42-43. It appears that there was a lot of pressure to keep silent about belief in Jesus, especially among the Pharisees (see p. 104). Why do you think this was so? What would have been the cost of making a public declaration of belief in Jesus?

21. Read John 16:31. Jesus says to His disciples, "You believe at last!" What were the disciples doing before this time? Disbelieving? Or do you think they were gradually growing in their belief? Why?

22. Mears makes the point that the message of Jesus will always divide the crowds (see p. 98). Some will believe; some will re-

ject. What does this mean for you regarding preaching and living out the gospel in the world? How do people's responses to your faith in Christ affect your willingness to share with others?

23. How should you respond if some people reject Jesus? What are the consequences of not sharing?

24. What is your personal responsibility for spreading the good news of Jesus?

Clarifying Salvation
Mears explains in further detail what people need to count on for salvation.

25. A lot of people think they are Christians simply because they are born into a Christian family or culture, or because their ethnic group is Christian, as opposed to Buddhist, Muslim

or polytheistic. What does John 1:13 say about this particular kind of thinking?

_____

_____

_____

_____

PUBLIC MINISTRY (JOHN 1:19–12)

Jesus' public ministry began when John the Baptist openly declared Jesus as the Messiah, the Lamb of God.

26. Jesus performed many signs and miracles to prove He was the Messiah. Read John 2:12-22. How is this scene a sign of Jesus' resurrection? How is the resurrection proof of Jesus' deity?

_____

_____

_____

_____

27. What other miracles did Jesus perform in John 3–11? What impact did they have on the people who believed? What impact do they have on you?

_____

_____

_____

_____

_____

PRIVATE MINISTRY (JOHN 13–17)

Henrietta Mears calls John 13–17 "the holy of holies of the Scriptures" (p. 105). The phrase "holy of holies" comes from the holiest part of the Temple—the place closed to the public and to which the high priest only went once a year in a terribly formal, solemn ceremony. It was where the Ark of the Covenant rested—the box built to hold artifacts from Israel's earliest history, over which two statues of angels hovered and where the manifest presence of God, the Shechinah Glory, would periodically shine.

28. Take some time to read Jesus' last instructions to His disciples in John 13–17. Why do you think Mears chose the phrase "holy of holies" to describe this section of John's Gospel?

29. There are many wonderful things Jesus teaches in John 13–17. What is the greatest promise of these chapters to you? (Hint: Read John 14:12,16-18,26; 15:26; 16:7.)

30. Why was it to the disciples' advantage that Jesus left (i.e., died on the cross)? Was it just to forgive them their sins or to send them to heaven after they died? Or was it for more? When the Holy Spirit is with you, who also is with you?

31. How does the Holy Spirit help the believer?

SUFFERING AND DEATH (JOHN 18–19)

32. Read John 18:1-9. Who is in control of this situation? What does this say about Jesus?

_____
_____
_____
_____
_____
_____

33. What did Jesus accomplish on the cross?

_____
_____
_____
_____
_____
_____

VICTORY OVER DEATH (JOHN 20–21)

34. Jesus emerged from death with a transformed physical body. Read John 20:24-28 and 21:15-17. How did Jesus encourage His disciples? How do these encounters encourage your faith? How do they encourage your willingness to serve Christ and fulfill the Great Comission?

_____
_____
_____
_____
_____

35. Jesus only had one requirement of Peter in order to serve Him: "Do you love me?" (John 21:15-17). What command does Je-

sus give to those who truly love Him (see verse 19)? How can you obey this command?

_____

_____

_____

_____

_____

_____

36. Under "Use the Three Keys," Mears tells us that Dr. Gordon suggested a wonderful truth regarding John 1:12. The "front-door key" that opens the door to a relationship with God "hangs right at the very front, outside, low down, within every child's reach" (p. 113). Isn't it great to know that you don't have to have a great intellect to be right with God? Even children can respond to the love of God. Do you know any children that you can share the gospel with today?

_____

_____

_____

_____

_____

37. Faith is the great key that flings the door of salvation wide open. If anyone can enter through faith, does this make Christian faith basically optimistic or pessimistic? What is your response of faith?

_____

_____

_____

_____

Note

1. John S. Spong, "A Call for a New Reformation," CCLEC Publications. http://www.episcopalian.org/cclec/paper-newreformation.htm.

Bible Reading Plans—One Year

ONE-YEAR PLAN
O.T. Books of Law and History

By the end of	Read Through	No. Pgs.
1st mo. ____	Genesis 37	____
2nd mo. ____	Exodus 25	____
3rd mo. ____	Leviticus 23	____
4th mo. ____	Numbers 28	____
5th mo. ____	Deuteronomy 30	____
6th mo. ____	Judges 8	____
7th mo. ____	1 Samuel 21	____
8th mo. ____	1 Kings 2	____
9th mo. ____	2 Kings 10	____
10th mo. ____	1 Chronicles 17	____
11th mo. ____	2 Chronicles 31	____
12th mo. ____	Esther 10	____

ONE-YEAR PLAN
O.T. Books of Poetry and Prophecy

By the end of	Read Through	No. Pgs.
1st mo. ____	Job 41	____
2nd mo. ____	Psalm 62	____
3rd mo. ____	Psalm 117	____
4th mo. ____	Proverbs 18	____
5th mo. ____	Isaiah 8	____
6th mo. ____	Isaiah 43	____
7th mo. ____	Jeremiah 6	____
8th mo. ____	Jeremiah 38	____
9th mo. ____	Ezekiel 15	____
10th mo. ____	Ezekiel 45	____
11th mo. ____	Amos 6	____
12th mo. ____	Malachi 4	____

ONE-YEAR PLAN
New Testament Books

By the end of	Read Through	No. Pgs.
1st mo. ____	Matthew 20	____
2nd mo. ____	Mark 8	____
3rd mo. ____	Luke 6	____
4th mo. ____	Luke 23	____
5th mo. ____	John 13	____
6th mo. ____	Acts 11	____
7th mo. ____	Romans 1	____
8th mo. ____	1 Corinthians 11	____
9th mo. ____	Ephesians 6	____
10th mo. ____	Philemon	____
11th mo. ____	2 Peter 3	____
12th mo. ____	Revelation 22	____

Bible Reading Plans—Two Year

TWO-YEAR PLAN
New Testament Books

By the end of	Read Through	No. Pgs.
1st mo.	Matthew 11	
2nd mo.	Matthew 20	
3rd mo.	Matthew 27	
4th mo.	Mark 8	
5th mo.	Mark 16	
6th mo.	Luke 6	
7th mo.	Luke 13	
8th mo.	Luke 23	
9th mo.	John 6	
10th mo.	John 13	
11th mo.	Acts 2	
12th mo.	Acts 11	
13th mo.	Acts 20	
14th mo.	Romans 1	
15th mo.	Romans 14	
16th mo.	1 Corinthians 11	
17th mo.	2 Corinthians 10	
18th mo.	Ephesians 6	
19th mo.	1 Thessalonians 5	
20th mo.	Philemon	
21st mo.	Hebrews 13	
22nd mo.	2 Peter 3	
23rd mo.	Revelation 8	
24th mo.	Revelation 22	

TWO-YEAR PLAN
O.T. Books of Poetry and Prophecy

By the end of	Read Through	No. Pgs.
1st mo.	Job 20	
2nd mo.	Job 41	
3rd mo.	Psalm 33	
4th mo.	Psalm 62	
5th mo.	Psalm 88	
6th mo.	Psalm 117	
7th mo.	Psalm 150	
8th mo.	Proverbs 18	
9th mo.	Ecclesiastes 7	
10th mo.	Isaiah 8	
11th mo.	Isaiah 27	
12th mo.	Isaiah 43	
13th mo.	Isaiah 59	
14th mo.	Jeremiah 6	
15th mo.	Jeremiah 23	
16th mo.	Jeremiah 38	
17th mo.	Jeremiah 52	
18th mo.	Ezekiel 15	
19th mo.	Ezekiel 29	
20th mo.	Ezekiel 45	
21st mo.	Daniel 12	
22nd mo.	Amos 6	
23rd mo.	Habakkuk 2	
24th mo.	Malachi 4	

TWO-YEAR PLAN
O.T. Books of Law and History

By the end of	Read Through	No. Pgs.
1st mo.	Genesis 21	
2nd mo.	Genesis 37	
3rd mo.	Exodus 6	
4th mo.	Exodus 25	
5th mo.	Leviticus 5	
6th mo.	Leviticus 23	
7th mo.	Numbers 11	
8th mo.	Numbers 28	
9th mo.	Deuteronomy 9	
10th mo.	Deuteronomy 30	
11th mo.	Joshua 14	
12th mo.	Judges 8	
13th mo.	1 Samuel 2	
14th mo.	1 Samuel 21	
15th mo.	2 Samuel 12	
16th mo.	1 Kings 2	
17th mo.	1 Kings 16	
18th mo.	2 Kings 10	
19th mo.	1 Chronicles 1	
20th mo.	1 Chronicles 17	
21st mo.	2 Chronicles 8	
22nd mo.	2 Chronicles 31	
23rd mo.	Nehemiah 3	
24th mo.	Esther 10	

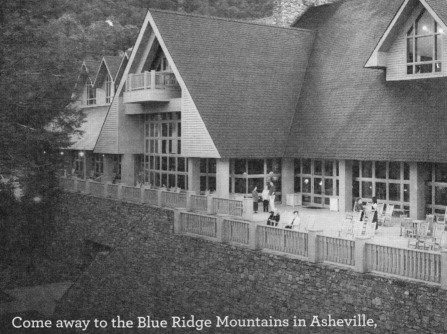

STEPS TO PEACE WITH GOD

1. RECOGNIZE GOD'S PLAN—PEACE AND LIFE

The message in this book stresses that God loves you and wants you to experience His peace and life.

The BIBLE says ... For God loved the world so much that He gave His only Son, so that everyone who believes in Him may not die but have eternal life. John 3:16

2. REALIZE OUR PROBLEM—SEPARATION FROM GOD

People choose to disobey God and go their own way. This results in separation from God.

The BIBLE says ... Everyone has sinned and is far away from God's saving presence. Romans 3:23

3. RESPOND TO GOD'S REMEDY—THE CROSS OF CHRIST

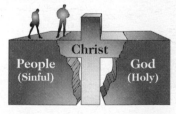

God sent His Son to bridge the gap. Christ did this by paying the penalty of our sins when He died on the cross and rose from the grave.

The BIBLE says ... But God has shown us how much He loves us—it was while we were still sinners that Christ died for us! Romans 5:8

4. RECEIVE GOD'S SON—LORD AND SAVIOR

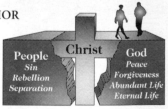

You cross the bridge into God's family when you ask Christ to come into your life.

The BIBLE says ... Some, however, did receive Him and believed in Him; so He gave them the right to become God's children. John 1:12

THE INVITATION IS TO:
REPENT (turn from your sins), ASK for God's forgiveness, and by faith RECEIVE Jesus Christ into your heart and life and follow Him in obedience as your Lord and Savior.

PRAYER OF COMMITMENT
"Dear Lord Jesus, I know that I am a sinner, and I ask for Your forgiveness. I believe You died for my sins and rose from the dead. I turn from my sins and invite You to come into my heart and life. I want to trust and follow You as my Lord and Savior. In Your Name, amen."

If you are committing your life to Christ, please let us know!

Billy Graham Evangelistic Association
1 Billy Graham Parkway, Charlotte, NC 28201-0001
1-877-2GRAHAM (1-877-247-2426)
BillyGraham.org/Commitment

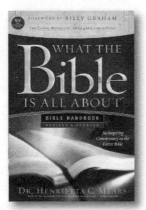
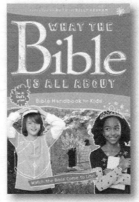
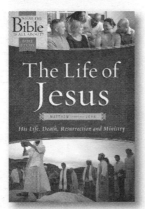
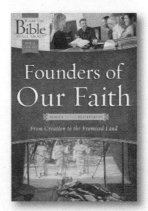